Sweet & Sorrow

Tanya Makes a Cookbook

Sweet & Sorrow

Tanya Makes a Cookbook

By Tanya Eby

BLUNDER
WOMAN
productions

Cover Art — Kim Hindman

Photos — Tanya Eby

Published by Blunder Woman Productions
Grand Rapids, MI

ISBN 978-1-7327337-5-6

Here's to friends, lovers,

and time alone

and here is do they fabulous Lynsey —
Happy Birthday.
Ben ♡

Contents

Warning xi
The Importance Of Snacks 3
The Cheese Puff That's Either A Curse Or A Blessing 4
Olive Cheese Ball Bites 6
Smoked Whitefish Dip 8
Crab Puffs 11
Cock Kabobs 14
Boozy Balls 17
Panzanella Salad 22
Bone Broth 25
Two Good Sandwiches 28
Muffuletta Sandwich 30
Now & Later Spinach Pie 32
To The Women I Have Loved And Lost 37
Broccoli (Chicken) Rice Casserole 42
White Chicken Chili 44
Grilled Shrimp Foil Packets 46
Instant Pot Butter Chicken 48
Polenta Fries And Bruschetta 50
Sesame Chicken 52
"I Want You To Fuck Me Before Dinner" Pasta 55
Homemade Pasta 57
Veggie Rice Breakfast Casserole 58
Tamale Pie 60
Mojo Pork 64

Old School Meatloaf 66
Recipe For Whatever 67
Polenta 70
Polenta Fries 71
Polenta Stuffed With Goat Cheese And Sun-Dried Tomatoes 72
Rice Salad 74
Veggie Cheese Cascade 76
Lentil Salad With Goat Cheese And Walnuts 77
Roasted Veggies 79
Focaccia 81
Fancy Grilled Cheese Sandwiches 84
White Bean Dip 86
Morels: Two Ways 88
Hangover Hash Browns 94
One Pot Brownies 100
Alexander Cake 102
Peanut Butter Cookies With Three Ingredients 103
These Are Anne Of Green Gables Tarts, Motherfuckers 104
Reddi-Wip From The Can 106
Every Day Is Sundae 107
Volcano Sundae 110
Beaver Cake 112
The Fucking Drink 116
Acknowledgments 119
About The Author 121

SWEET & SORROW

Warning

I want to start off with a little true story here, just before you get too far into this. Just so we can come to a sort of understanding between us.

I am now going to tell you one of the very embarrassing things that happened while I was in New York City this week. It's taken me three days to work up the courage to share this with you.

After a very long day in a board meeting for #Audiobooks, I was brain dead, overwhelmed and more than a little hungry. I stumbled into my hotel's restaurant at 4PM hoping to buy a big glass of wine and, I dunno, an entire cow to eat.

But they weren't serving dinner yet. Luckily, the waiter told me that it was Happy Hour. And there were snacks.

"Oh, snacks!" I said with glee. I could make a MEAL out of snacks. So I ordered my GG&T (Ginger gin & tonic), got my drink and waited for my snacks.

I drank the drink. Mmmm. Things were better. BUT THERE WERE NO SNACKS. That was odd. I noticed a buffet in the back of the restaurant. Ah! That's where the snacks were. I would make those snacks mine. I approached. There were these strange burritos and no silverware.

That's okay. Maybe it was a Millennial thing. Who needs silverware for a burrito? Who needed a plate? This was a Portable Snack.

I grabbed the burrito (sans plate) and went to my table.

The burrito, dear reader, was hard. Did I eat it anyway?

Yes.

Yes. I did.

It was stuffed with chewy meat and some sort of cheese like product. Not good. Worst Happy Hour snack ever! It took a solid thirty seconds of chewing before I could get that first bite down. The second bite took even longer.

Then the manager approached.

"I'm so sorry, dear lady, but you seem to have consumed our employee meal that was inadvertently left out since lunch, about 4 hours ago. I'm sorry for any misunderstanding."

I just blinked at him. And offered a little burp.

Dammit! I ATE THE EMPLOYEES' BURRITO! The hard, chewy meat burrito that had been sitting out there FOREVER. And the worst thing…the worst WORST thing…I sort of wanted another one.

#sigh

#BlunderWomanStrikesAgain

#ButYouSaidThereWereSnacks

You see…this is the person who is about to write things for you to use, and possibly sometimes even give advice to you. In no way should you put your faith in me. Take everything I say with a grain of salt. Not even that. Take it with a grain of air.

Remember, I call myself Blunder Woman online for a reason.

I am the woman who ate a four-hour-old rock-hard burrito because the waiter promised me snacks.

The Importance Of Snacks

I love food. All sorts of food. You know how you have days when you want to hear a certain song or a certain type of music? Maybe it's a cool rainy day and you want classical music with like harps and shit. Maybe it's a hot, bright day in July and only Yacht Rock will do.

There's a song for your mood. It's the same with food.

And goddammit if I didn't just rhyme.

I'm an emotional eater. Most people say this apologetically, but I'm not saying it in that tone. I'm embracing it. I'm saying, "Hell yeah! I'm an emotional eater! Because there is the perfect dish for every mood." Is this healthy? Fuck you!

Sorry. I didn't mean to get angry with you.

I just mean to say, gently and lovingly, that being an emotional eater shouldn't be a bad thing. There is a food that can enhance or soothe every mood. And sometimes, not eating is just the thing you need. Now, I'm not condoning drowning your sorrows and loneliness in a pint of ice cream and a family size bag of potato chips…if you're doing that every day. But you know, sometimes life is so shitty and you just need comfort from the inside out. Something's that sweet and salty and just plain awful for you snack, is exactly what you need. And you'll take that in and mourn, wail, feel awful, regret all your life choices, and then tomorrow…you'll do things differently.

If that's your mood, if that's what you need, do the thing.

And tomorrow, eat a salad and do some yoga.

That's Om Life, motherfuckers.

At any rate, I wanted to talk about snacks. And I also want to talk about main meals, and sandwiches, and soups, and desserts. I want to talk about sex, and loneliness, and sexy loneliness. I might also want to talk about poetry. But not very much because poetry is mostly too smart for me.

I guess what I'm saying here is what you are about to read is a mishmash of just WHATEVER. But I hope it's a bit of a love song too. A love song to friendships, to lovers, to being solitary. To those dark, cold moods, and those moods where you feel like you have birthed a star within you and it is shining forth.

I guess what this is all about is life. In all its sweet and sorrow.

I mean, sweet and sour.

Although, honestly, sweet and sorrow works well too.

The Cheese Puff That's Either A Curse Or A Blessing

Story Interlude

I want to tell you about the worst party I ever attended. The party was fine, actually, but I made it the worst party ever.

It was a Christmas party. Think: snow in Michigan. That kind of blue glow outside where it's dark, but it's also a sort of light because the snow has created this weird softening of sound and light.

My roommate and I were invited to a party. We were both single and both introverts, and I'm not even sure how we were invited to this party. I think it was through a theater person we knew. We donned our party gear. K had long dark hair, bright blue eyes, and dressed in silk and velvet. She looked like the cover model of a 1930s magazine. I had a regrettable haircut because I thought that bangs would solve all my problems.

The bangs solved nothing.

I smooshed my thighs into some corduroy pants and put on a comfy sweater. When I walked in the snow, you could hear my thighs rubbing together a mile away. K. assured me they were Statement Pants. They went with my bangs, I guess.

We entered the party.

I was expecting the typical theater party with people standing in a circle giving each other sub-par massages, and a couple in the corner doing their best Monty Python imitations. There'd be a table with snacks. Chips and salsa. A few bags of softening Taco Bell tacos. A bowl of candy leftover from opening night.

This was not that party.

At this party there was slow jazz playing. Christmas music, I think. People stood around talking quietly in their socks. The appetizers were on burners and had labels. One of them looked like a stuffed cockroach, but I later discovered it was a date.

Everyone at this party had a meaningful job. They were lawyers and doctors. There were therapists and teachers. I know this because they were all talking about their work.

I was gainfully employed, but I never talked about it. Instead, I talked about being a Writer. Oh, you know, I'm a playwright, I'd say. My last show sold out! (It was a black box performance and we had twenty seats and a cast of ten, so that wasn't a surprise we sold out.)

K immediately found a comfortable corner to hide in, but I decided to just bust into the party and introduce myself.

"Hey!" I said. "I'm Tanya!"

They all looked at me. Collectively blinked. Then someone said, "What do you do, Tanya?"

The room suddenly quieted. Pure silence, except for the snow outside. I couldn't tell them I was a writer. They didn't want to hear about my creative endeavors. They wanted to know about my professional life. I could do this! I had a profession. "I work at Gilda's Club!" I said enthusiastically. I was in charge of development and fundraising there.

"What's Gilda's Club?" someone asked.

"Oh! We're a cancer support community. I help raise money for people with cancer."

I didn't think the party could get much quieter, but it did. Then someone said, "My mom just died of cancer," and she started crying.

Then a bunch of other people started crying. Her mom was really popular. Then someone admitted they had cancer and didn't know how to process it. Then a therapist jumped in to talk about dying.

The whole place became a shitshow.

I looked at K smiling darkly in the corner.

"Merry Christmas!" I said.

And we left.

This is why I don't go to parties.

But if I did go, I'd bring Olive Cheese Ball Bites.

Olive Cheese Ball Bites

I'm pretty sure these treats were created in the 1950's. I have no data to support that, it's just it feels like the sort of thing you'd have in the fifties. I can imagine a plate of these sitting next to a wiggling Jell-O mold, and Ritz crackers sprayed with cheese product.

Don't be misled, though. These balls are delicious. They're crispy, salty, cheese, with that bite of the olive.

Plus, you'll have a great time rolling these balls around your palm.

Stuff You Need

- 2 cups shredded cheddar cheese
- 1 cup all-purpose flour
- 1/8 tsp onion powder
- 1/8 tsp garlic powder
- 1/2 cup melted butter
- 1 jar green olives with pimento

What You Do

1. Mix everything together (except the olives). It'll form a kind of a clumpy dough. Take about a tablespoon of the dough, flatten it in your hand till it resembles a disc, and then place a shiny green olive at its center. Then you pinch the dough around the olive.
2. Now for the fun part. Roll that ball in the palms of your hands. Make it nice and round. Your ball will be slightly misshapen, but that's okay. A slightly misshapen ball tastes just fine. If you're really good, you can shape two balls at once! I've never been able to do that. I just don't have the focus.
3. Once you have all the balls made, refrigerate for about an hour. If you don't, you won't have balls. You'll have bare-naked olives with a sad party dress of cheese sloughed off.
4. Heat oven to 400°. Bake for 15-20 minutes, until there's a slight browning. I find it's best to taste test at this point for quality control, and also to make sure the dough isn't gooey. It should be firm-ish on the outside but soft on the inside. I end up doing a lot of testing.

A lot.

There you go! Olive Cheese Ball Bites! Perfect for that retro party. Serve with martinis, pineapple and water chestnuts wrapped in bacon, a cheese ball, and marinated mozzarella on sticks and… I could on and on.

Play the game and see which of your friends are cursed or blessed.Don't tell them there's an olive in there. When they bite it, if they like olives, they're blessed. If they hate olives, they're cursed. If they're cursed, hug them, then tell them to get the fuck out. Because who doesn't like olives?

Smoked Whitefish Dip

When You Want To Be All Fancy And Shit

There are times when you want to impress people. I get it. I do. I feel this way 100% of the time. When I'm PMS-ing, it's 110% of the time.

Here is a recipe where you can tell your friends you made this incredible dip with crudités and fresh bread, and it's such a burden being so amazing in the kitchen.

Here's the thing though.

I tried to make this recipe. I did. For my YouTube video series *Tanya Makes.*

I got real smoked whitefish. "Fresh from Lake Michigan!" the sign read. It smelled like smoke and fish so I knew it was good.

I flaked that fish off the bone, massaged it in between my fingers. I tossed it, lightly, lovingly, with mayonnaise and lemon juice and capers. I sprinkled in parsley. I put it on a platter with fresh baked bread and fancy carrot sticks.

I was brilliant. I was a domestic goddess!

All would worship at my feet!

And then I tried it.

IT WAS FUCKING HORRIBLE!

Worst bite of smoky ass fish I've ever had. The spoonful I tried had a part of bone in it, and it was glistening indecently. GLISTENING I tells ya. And that is just plain wrong.

Here, then, is my amended recipe for Smoked Whitefish Dip.

Stuff You Need

1 container Whitefish Dip

What You Do

1. Just go to the fucking store and buy it.
2. Spoon it out, fluff it, and put it in a pretty pottery bowl.
3. Surround it with fresh bread you purchased from a bakery and crudités someone else cut for you at the deli.
4. Tell your friends you didn't fucking make anything.
5. Eat the dip and laugh and laugh and laugh.
6. Your friends will fall at your feet in worship, because this is how real domestic goddesses operates: they know their limits. They put their time and energy into things that really matter. Like martinis.

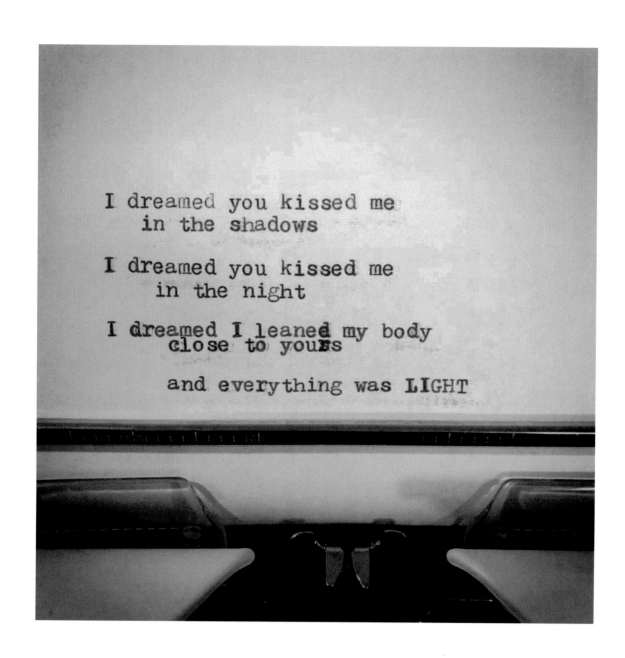

I dreamed you kissed me
in the shadows

I dreamed you kissed me
in the night

I dreamed I leaned my body
close to yours

and everything was LIGHT

Crab Puffs

When You Want To Seem Fancy And Actually Cook Something But Really, It's Just Puff Pastry

There are lots of days when I want to feel fancy, usually after I've had a pedicure and my feet are all pretty and smooth and far from the Hobbit feet they usually are. And then I want to put on a bathrobe to highlight my pretty feet, sip a glass of wine, and eat something fancy.

Most of the time I'm too lazy to actually put in the work of something fancy, so this recipe is perfect for that.

You can cook it while drinking wine and wearing a bathrobe. Eat it all alone while bingeing on a foreign series on Netflix, or just watch The Bachelor with the subtitles on.

If you want to involve friends or your loved one or someone you just want to love ON for the evening, by all means. This is your party.

You are so fancy.

Stuff You Need

- 8 oz. Lump Crab Meat. (It can be real or fake. If fake, release it from the vacuum bag and fluff it with a fork so it at least resembles real crab meat.)
- 6 oz. Cream Cheese, softened (Cream Cheese is sold in 8 oz packages so either cream cheese it up and add more, or save the rest of the cheese to smear on your bagel. Or whatever you smear cream cheese onto.)
- 1 tablespoon Mayonnaise. (Get the real stuff or I'll punch you in the throat.)
- 1 clove Garlic, minced (You can also use garlic powder because mincing is work.)
- ½ tsp Worcestershire (Use whilst trying to say Worcestershire)
- ½ tsp Soy Sauce
- 1 Green Onion, chopped
- 2 sheets Pepperidge Farm Puff Pastry, thawed
- Salt and pepper

What You Do

1. Preheat oven to 400°.
2. In a medium bowl, mix together everything but the puff pastry. If you try to mix in the puff pastry, that shit's on you. I don't understand you. But it's okay. Maybe the dog will eat it.
3. Flour the countertop and roll out a sheet of pastry to a 10" x 15" rectangle. Or whatever. You can get your ruler out or you can kinda just lightly tap the roller on the dough and say "There! I did it!" Try to flatten it out a bit. Why? BECAUSE YOU'LL GET MORE SNACKS OUT OF IT.
4. You can start with just the one sheet of pastry and see if you want to make more. I usually do.
5. Using a pizza cutter or knife slice into 2½" squares. Again, you can measure, or you can just slice into whatever size you think you can ram into a mini muffin tin and still have a little on the edges.
6. Place one square in each well of a mini muffin tray.
7. Add one tablespoon crab mixture into each cup. For me, a tablespoon of mixture is just whatever looks like it sits well in the pastry.

Bake for 20-25 minutes or until puff pastry is golden. That seems like a long time, but fancy things take time.

Top with green onions if you want to be super fancy and serve immediately. But don't eat it immediately. I tried that and burned my mouth. So, serve immediately, but get comfy on your couch with the right blankets, queue up whatever you're watching, have a mini makeout session, admire your feet, and THEN eat them.

Cock Kabobs

I found this recipe in an old 1950s cookbook. The kind of cookbook that calls for a lot of canned soup and meat products. Luckily, this recipe doesn't have either of those things. It does have cocktail wieners though, so that's a plus.

Consider serving these at a book club gathering. That way you can talk about cock kabobs and laugh and laugh and laugh. Of course, because it's a book club, you'll be drunk, so that will make it even funnier.

Stuff You Need

1 cup flour
1/2 teaspoon salt
1/ 3 cup shortening
1/4 cup grated American
  or Cheddar cheese
2 to 4 TBS water
Cocktail sausages (cut in
  half)
Olives
toothpicks

What You Do

1. Heat oven to 475°.
2. In a bowl, and not just on the counter (you're not a monster), mix the flour and salt. Cut in shortening. Blend in cheese. Sprinkle on water, and mix with a fork. Round into ball. If you can't round it into a ball, you might want to add more water. You may also want to add a little bit more salt.
3. Pat dough into a disc shape and roll 1/8 inch thick, the way you would make pie crust. Cut into 1" rounds. (I used the cap on a water bottle, and it made the perfect little round spheres.)
4. Alternate weenie with dough and olives on a toothpick, kabob style. Lay on foil covered cookie sheet. Bake 10 to 12 minutes or until pastry is lightly brown. Serve with cocktail sauce.

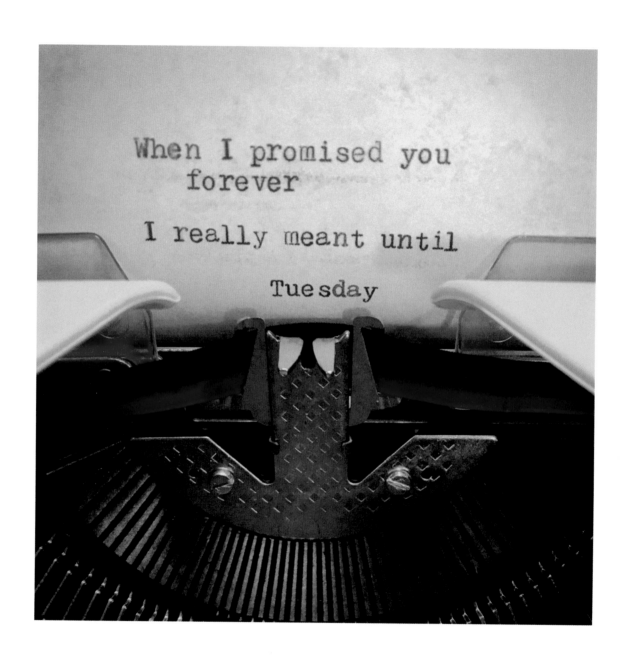

Boozy Balls

When You Want To Be Silly

I was traumatized by a pair of balls when I was little. And I blame it all on my brother. When I was ten or something and he was fourteen, he was wearing these cutoff jeans shorts. They were cut so short you could see the pockets hanging out. One day he was climbing a tree and I was below him being an annoying little sister, and I saw something weird and red flecked with hair sort of squish out by his leg. He was either birthing an alien, or it was something worse. Cancer maybe. Or the strangest blister I'd ever seen. I did what any young sister would do. I pointed and screamed.

Then he educated me and told me they were just balls and to shut up and go inside.

I can still feel the horror.

The first balls I ever touched happened in high school. Well, not IN high school, but after school. I was a senior and dated the high school quarterback for about ten minutes. He introduced me to Pearl Jam and Nirvana and we'd talk about poetry and stuff. He asked me to hang out with him, so I did. Because I felt enormous pressure from everyone to date and kiss and be sexual in some way, after school, I slipped my hand down his pants while we were watching TV. I didn't know what to do, so I just…held him. Didn't move or anything. Just sort of cupped one of his balls and waited. "Uhm, Tanya?" He asked. "What are you doing?"

After a time, I said, "I'm. Not. Really. Sure."

We broke up shortly after that.

Later, in college, I decided that balls weren't such a bad thing after all. They were still alien and all, but they weren't life threatening or anything.

And now…with this life journey I have made, I still laugh at the idea of balls. Every time I make olive cheese balls, or meatballs, or boozy balls, I just giggle. Because. Balls.

It's a good thing I don't have them. I'd never take myself seriously.

I made these for *Tanya Makes* and I had a recipe. I really did. But then I made all these substitutions because I didn't have pear juice or flavored vodka…and by the time I was done, my recipe was completely different than the actual one. And I didn't measure anything. It was a hot day and I started out by mixing vodka and pineapple juice and Orange Curaçao and testing it for a while before I added in a bunch of watermelon balls, so let's say I was pretty much lit when I actually got those balls in.

Here's what you do, basically:

Make your balls. You now know how I feel about balls. They're ridiculous and fun; and nice to sometimes just sit there and hold. The Making of The Balls is the most important part of the recipe. Make them with a melon scoop and you can just do watermelon, which I did, or cantaloupe, honeydew, whatever.

Pour those balls into a big hollowed out bowl (like a watermelon corpse) and then layer in a shit ton of vodka, pineapple juice, and curacao. Or whatever you have on hand that tastes good together. Stir it up. Cover with Saran Wrap and chill for a few hours or until you forget about it. The more it sits, the boozier it gets. Then you're ready to eat!

I poured the excess juice out into a pitcher and drank that over ice. So good.

And check this out: you can freeze the balls, put them in a blender later, and you'll have an instant boozy smoothie!!

God. This recipe is amazing. I don't know why I'm still here writing. I need to go make these again. I'm going to make these and then eat them while watching 90 Day Fiancé, because this is living the good life.

Lunch

My favorite lunch was Chipped Beef when I was growing up. We'd buy these bags of sliced lunch meat. They were $0.29 or four for a dollar. My mom showed me how to cook it: you'd put butter and flour in a pan, stir it a little, add some milk, and then add in your meat, and then pour it over a piece of toast.

This idea terrifies me now, but I loved it as a kid. One, because I didn't know any better, and two, because we were actually really poor and there just weren't a lot of options.

My favorite dinner was Swanson's fried chicken with corn, mashed potatoes, and a brownie. The classic TV dinner. I still crave it.

Lunch over the years has always confused me a little bit. In my understanding "Lunch" is anything that happens after breakfast, so somewhere between 9:30 AM and 2:00 PM. It's also always a little disappointing. Lunch is something that wants to be dinner.

Lunch is the thing you eat in between working where you either feel guilty because everything was deep fried, or you feel good because you ate a salad and you're still ravenous. In my opinion, lunch is stupid.

But it doesn't have to be! Lunch doesn't have to be something to fill the gap in your hunger. Lunch is an opportunity!

You can eat something hearty. Something that feels good and is maybe fried or not. Lunch shouldn't be a throw away like a granola bar and some warm string cheese shoved into your gaping maw because you just don't have time for anything else.

Make time.

We only have so many meals in this lovely life. Make them count.

And if Chipped Beef is your thing, make that. You have the power here.

Here are some of my favorite lunches. Sometimes I explain why, but sometimes I don't feel like explaining anything and I just don't.

I'm moody that way.

Panzanella Salad

When You Just Need Bread & Cheese

I will be honest with you because I am always honest with you, because it is easy to be honest when you're writing a cookbook while drinking a fruity rum drink and eating a Cubano sandwich.

This salad is my favorite salad in the whole word, narrowly beating out the Salad Lyonnaise I had in Paris with my husband when we were on our honeymoon and everything was romantic. This is my favorite salad because 1) there's actually no salad (lettuce) in it and 2) It's mostly just bread and cheese. It's also my favorite because this salad does not speak French to you when you're hungry and you can't understand anything or read anything because everything is foreign so you just stand in the middle of the street and tears start pouring down your face because you just want bread and cheese and how the fuck do you say that in French when you don't speak French and you're basically a walking buffoon?

(Pausing for a second, because I am breathing heavily.)

Ahem.

Let me try that again.

What is more beautiful than crispy, salty croutons, sweet tomatoes, creamy cheese, and a little bite of balsamic vinegar? Besides receiving cunnilingus, because nothing, honestly, is better than that. What's better? NOTHING.

This is a terrific salad. Make it. Eat it all the time. Breakfast, lunch, dinner. On a Sunday. On a Tuesday. Make it for friends. Horde it for yourself. It doesn't matter. Just make it. Eat it. Savor it.

Stuff You Need

Crusty French bread (or any bread
    really)
Olive oil
Salt and pepper
Fresh mozzarella, chopped or
    those little balls you can buy
Good tomatoes
Balsamic vinegar
Basil (Optional)

What You Do

1. Preheat oven to 425°.
2. Slice some French bread and then cut into cubes. How much? I don't know. How much do you want to eat? Shoot for two big handfuls. But man-handfuls. Not dainty tiny handfuls. Put cubed bread in a bowl. Drizzle with olive oil. How much? Drizzle some over the top until it looks good. Then add some more. Season with salt and pepper and toss. Taste one piece of bread. If it's a little salty and a little oily, it's perfect.
3. Bake in preheated oven for about five minutes or until it's a nice golden color. Let cool.
4. When you're ready to eat, toss croutons with cheese and tomatoes, about equal quantities of each. Drizzle with balsamic vinegar and olive oil. Top with some chopped basil.

When you eat, slow down for a minute and really EAT it. Smell it, savor it, taste it. Eat the croutons with your fingers. This is a simple and decadent salad. Take time to BE there when you eat it.

Bone Broth

When You Need To Eat Something, Anything But You're Grieving

My darling, I'm writing this to you, but it's also to me.

I had a shitty childhood. I really did. We all did. I'm not saying mine was shittier, but it was shitty just enough. There was poverty, and mental illness, and abandonment, and abuse, and sadness, oh such sadness. There was loss and pain and there were times where I did not know if I would be safe, or alive. Even after I grew up and moved on, this childhood clung to me with cold claws and weighed me down.

What I needed growing up, was someone to love me. To cradle me. To wrap me in warmth and say, "There, there. Life is hard and it is not fair but you will make it through this."

What I needed was the emotional equivalent to a bowl of homemade soup.

Sometimes, we all need that: warmth, love, comfort, nourishment.

There will be times in your life when the world is not fair to you. When unjust things happen. When you try your hardest to be good, and right, and healthy, and connected, and positive, and upbeat, but still…something terrible happens.

There will be times where you're heartbroken. Exhausted. Penniless. Afraid. So worn out that all you can do is cry and cry and cry. There will be times when you are ill. Maybe just a little ill, but maybe a bigger kind of ill. Ill in body, or ill in spirit, or maybe a little bit of both.

You won't want to eat during these times.

And that's okay.

For a bit.

But then you must eat. You must. Because you have to get up. For as long as you can, you have to get up.

I speak from experience. I've walked through so many of these moments. And if I haven't walked it, my friends or loved ones have.

Sometimes, the universe does things to you that are beyond your control and all you can do is rage, and cry, and become numb, and then get up and start your next day. And you keep starting your next day until one day, you've healed enough to smile.

This is grief.

It punches you. Sometimes you respond with tears. Sometimes with pure rage. Sometimes it confirms your thoughts that the world is an ugly place.

But the world is also a beautiful place.

Sometimes the world is both ugly and beautiful at the same time.

Ride through it. Feel it. Be mad. Be fierce. Be foul. Be heartbroken. Be tear filled. Be silent. Be rage.

But then, eventually, be free. Let go.

May this simple dish help you heal from the inside out. And may you find the comfort you deserve.

This recipe is for an Instant Pot, but you can make it the old-fashioned way and just let this simmer on the stove all day long. Your house will smell so comforting and loved.

Unless you're a vegetarian, then you probably just want to sip some hot water with lemon. That's healing too.

Stuff You Need

- 1 rotisserie chicken (use all the skin and bones. Save the meat for something else. You can also use a cut up raw chicken, skin and all)
- 1 cup baby carrots (the ones that sit in your fridge and that you promised you'll eat, but you never do)

Celery stalk, leaves and all

One onion, peeled and quartered

2 bay leaves

2 cloves garlic

Some thyme (½ tsp)

2 tsps of salt or powdered chicken stock (You need the salt. You do. Salt is flavor.)

10 Cups water (or to the FILL line)

What You Do

1. Put everything in your Instant Pot. Make sure it's set to sealing. Press SOUP/BROTH button (or high steam) and cook for 180 minutes.
2. You can cook for as little as 40 minutes, but the longer this bone broth simmers, the better it will be.
3. Release the steam before unlocking the top.
4. Put a large pot in the sink, top with a colander and pour the broth into it. You're straining out all the bones and veggies. They've done their job.
5. You can have a mug of broth on its own. It's calming and soothes your throat and belly. Or you can take a couple of cups of it, add ramen noodles and some chicken and bok choy for a ramen bowl.
6. When you chill the broth, it should have a little wiggle to it when it's totally cool. This means some of the collagen in the chicken broke down. That's what is so good for your skin and bones and spirit.
7. Freeze bags of the broth in single servings for later use.

Use whenever you need to soothe or calm your spirit.

Or make a really killer soup from it.

Things are starting to look up.

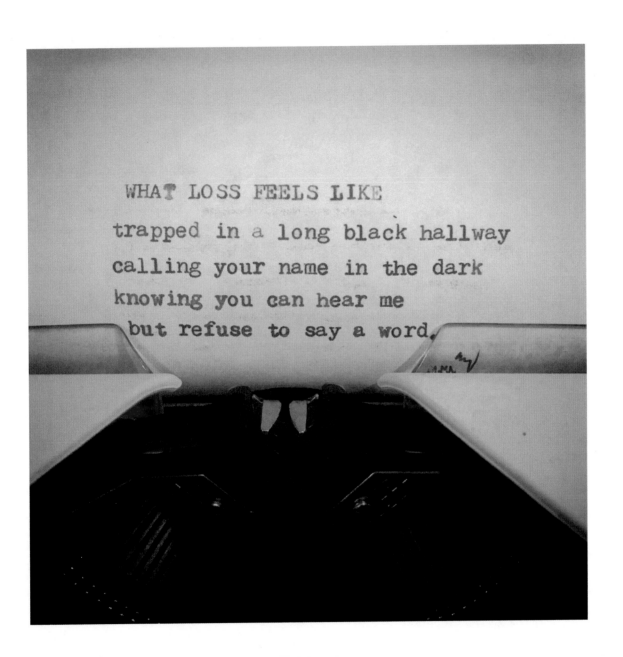

WHAT LOSS FEELS LIKE

trapped in a long black hallway
calling your name in the dark
knowing you can hear me
but refuse to say a word.

Two Good Sandwiches

When You Want Good Food But You Work From Home And Aren't Dressed

I want to get into the recipes here, but I also want to tell you why I think sandwiches are the best thing ever invented.

Why Sandwishes Are The Best Thing Ever Invented

By Tanya Eby

Age 7

Sandwishes are the bestest things ever! Because they are so good!

The end

Hmmm. I don't see a whole lot of promise in little Tanya Eby, age 7, except that she spelled "sandwiches" as "sandwishes" and maybe that's sort of brilliant.

I don't really know when or how my obsession began with sandwiches. I think it was probably in college, where I discovered sour dough bread and goat cheese and that an orgasm could be delivered to you by another person. Such wonders!

A good sandwich has a blend of all flavors: salty, sweet, bitter, sour and umami. But they're also a blend of all the textures: crispy, soft, smooth, gooey. And then there's a harmony of color: brown bread, black olive, green lettuce, white cheese, red tomato, yellow mustard. Or some variation of that. Sandwiches are a wish come true that you can carry around with you.

I think it's the whole balance thing that really sends me. Harmony and balance are soothing to the spirit, my spirit in particular because I spend 99% of my day feeling anxious. A good sandwich hits my soul deep and calms me, the way that someone brushing my hair calms me. It's more than food. It's nourishment.

Here, then, are a couple of sandwiches you can do at home…

Did you know…you can actually make a Cuban Sandwich at home! It's true! And you can make a Reuben Sandwich, and sliders, and or a Turkey Rueben or whatever you want AT HOME! It takes, like, 5 minutes and you'll feel so good because you didn't have to change out of your bathrobe to get lunch.

Cuban Sandwich

When you go grocery shopping on the weekend, think ahead a little. Pick up some good sour-dough bread, deli ham, deli turkey, dill pickle slices and swiss cheese. When you are home and hungry, slather two pieces of bread with mayo, open it up and slather with mustard. Put a slice of Swiss cheese on each side. Add pickle slices, ham, turkey, and if you've REALLY thought ahead, use some of your leftover Mojo Pork. Then treat the sandwich like a grilled cheese. Grill each side until golden. Press down on it with a spatula while cooking so everything gets smooshed and amazing. I zap my sandwiches in the microwave for 30 seconds before serving, to ensure gooey-ness.

Sometimes, I wait and put the pickle on so things don't get soggy. This is totally up to you. Maybe you like things a little limp.

Reuben Sandwich

This is the same process, but different ingredients. Get yourself some rye or pumpernickel bread (which is great as your morning toast too, because flavor), some corned beef or turkey, swiss or provolone cheese, sauerkraut, and Thousand Island dressing. Smear your bread with mayonnaise, layer the insides with all of your fixings, grill and press down, heat in microwave for 30 seconds.

Sometimes I make this open-faced where I put a slice of cheese on each bread slice and some deli meat. I grill the bread until the cheese is melted, THEN I add the sauerkraut and the dressing. This avoids the sog factor.

Muffuletta Sandwich

I can't say enough about this sandwich. I'm actually writing this in New Orleans right now.

It's seven in the morning, and the city is still deep asleep. It's hot and moist outside. Also, a man just told me I had great tits and that scared me so I retreated to the hotel lobby. Although I am proud too. What he said was true. I do have great tits.

Kids love these sandwiches too, so it's great to make these the night ahead of time, and they can grab them for lunches. Or if you have a beach day, make these and bring these sandwiches with you in a cooler. There are endless places you can take your sandwich.

There's a big debate out there about what makes an 'authentic' New Orleans Muffuletta. Lots of recipes call for peppers etc. And you can waste time and energy debating what goes into the perfect sandwich, or you can just make the damn sandwich, eat it, and then the next time you make it, try making it a little different until you come up with your perfect sandwich.

This is my perfect sandwich.

You can try to use a New Orleans accent while eating. But maybe swallow first before talking.

Stuff You Need

1/4 cup red wine vinegar
2 garlic cloves, peeled and minced
1 tsp dried oregano
1/3 cup olive oil
1/3 cup pitted green olives, chopped
1/3 cup pitted, chopped kalamata olives
1/4 cup chopped roasted red bell peppers
Salt and freshly ground black pepper
1 (1 lb) round bread loaf (about 7 inches in diameter and 3 inches high) OR you can make individual sandwiches using good rolls that have a little chew to them. Not super soft rolls.

4 ounces thinly sliced ham
4 ounces thinly sliced turkey
4 ounces thinly sliced salami
4 ounces sliced provolone
1/2 red onion, thinly sliced (Optional. I option out of this because I hate raw onions.)
1-1/2 ounces arugula leaves (Optional. I opt in when I can because it adds a little spice, but it can make the sandwich a little soggy long term.)

What You Do

1. Whisk the first 3 ingredients in a large bowl to blend. Gradually blend in the oil. Stir in the olives and roasted peppers. Season the vinaigrette, to taste, with salt and pepper.
2. Cut the top 1-inch of the bread loaf. Set the top aside. Hollow out the bottom and top halves of the bread.
3. Spread some of the olive and roasted pepper mix over the bread bottom and cut side of the bread top. Layer the meats and cheeses in the bread bottom.
4. Top with the onions, then the arugula.
5. Spread the remaining olive and roasted pepper mix on top of the sandwich and carefully cover with the bread top.
6. Cut the sandwich into wedges and serve.

You can serve the sandwich immediately or you can wrap the entire sandwich tightly in plastic wrap and place in the refrigerator a day before serving.

Now & Later Spinach Pie

When You Want Leftovers That Taste Fresh

This recipe makes two spinach pies: one to bake right away, and the other to freeze for later. You can easily half the recipe for just one pie. I get the feta at a membership warehouse club where it's a lot cheaper than at a regular store. Phyllo is in the freezer section in most grocery stores.

Stuff You Need

1/2 cup plus 2 tablespoons olive oil

4 medium onions, chopped

6 garlic cloves, minced

Salt and pepper

6 packages (10 oz. each) frozen, chopped spinach, thawed and squeezed dry

1 pound feta cheese, crumbled

1/2 cup grated Parmesan

1/2 cup dried breadcrumbs

2 tsp dried dill

8 large eggs, beaten

8 oz frozen phyllo sheets, thawed, and thinly sliced

What You Do

Preheat Oven to 375°

MAKE THE FILLING

1. In a large, nonstick pan, heat 2 tablespoons oil over medium-high heat. Add onions and cook, stirring occasionally, until translucent, 3-5 minutes. Add garlic and sprinkle with salt; cook until garlic is tender, about 1-2 minutes.
2. Transfer mixture to a large bowl; stir in spinach, feta, Parmesan, breadcrumbs, dill, salt and pepper to taste. Fold in the eggs until combined.
3. Divide mixture evenly between two 9-inch springform pans, or two deep-dish pie plates; press firmly to flatten.

MAKE THE TOPPING

1. In a large bowl, gently toss sliced phyllo to separate, then toss with remaining ½ cup oil until coated.
2. Divide between pies, covering the tops evenly. (To freeze, cover pie tightly with saran wrap, being careful not to flatten the topping. Bake within 3 months; do not thaw first.

Bake until heated through and topping is golden brown, about 30 minutes for unfrozen pie, 1 hour 15 minutes for frozen pie.

Interlude

A thought on Friends

I have this little maudlin piece I want to share with you and I've been trying to think of where to put it, but I can't figure out where it belongs, so I'm just putting it HERE. Now. Because why not?

I think about friends a lot, and I'm hoping this little book will be something one friend can give to another. Not just because of potential sales, but because it's honestly nice to do something for someone your care about, especially when they aren't expecting it.

Here then, is a little something I wrote for the women friends I've had in my life. And there's a little bit about food in here, because there is always a little bit about food.

To The Women I Have Loved And Lost

Kaly was my first love. Our Barbies humped in her room upstairs, her house slouching next to a gas station. We made dresses for the Barbies and they were fashion queens; and then when Ken came in, everything went to hell. I didn't know then that I was creating a pattern in my life. Ken, the bastard, would always tear friendships apart.

Then there was Katie. She had blonde hair like Sally in Charlie Brown. She wore plastic bangle bracelets, slouchy shirts, and puffy skirts. She played the piano while I sang Barry Manilow. We watched Madonna on MTV. We sang so loud we had to open the windows so our song could escape.

Missy lived across the street and we felt pressure to be friends because our moms were friends. I sat in her room and we listened to 45s. She played "I'm Your Venus" but I thought it was "I'm Your Penis" and I refused to sing it out loud, but wouldn't tell her why.

I moved and my friends could not come with me. They slipped silently underwater.

At my new school and now living with my dad and his wife and my new stepsiblings, I fumbled around for a good friend. My stepsister would become my life's greatest love, and one of the most complicated. We went through everything together: first period, first crushes, first heartbreaks. We snuck out once in the middle of summer to meet a couple of boys at the basketball court, but it was boring and we snuck home. We shared a bed and sometimes we'd kick each other, trying to hurt the other one. She lit her bangs on fire and we laughed and laughed at how fast Aqua Net could ignite. Boys loved her. Boys thought I was her brother. I dreamed of being beautiful, like her. (I still dream this.)

High school friends were on the outside of my life, but in my senior year, there was Kim and Cheryl, the Cheerleader and the Brain. We took an independent study with Mr. Messing. One day, we spread out a blanket on the front lawn and I made them listen to Crosby, Stills, & Nash even though this was our parents' music. We listened and we talked of all the places we would go. How we were unlikely friends, but our lives would be magical.

In college, I had roommates. Amy with the wild hair, so curly it seemed like it was trying to escape from her head. And Jill, who was eight years older, a returning student. She drank her coffee with a straw because she didn't want to have yellow teeth. Shannon wanted to be a doctor. I didn't understand her. She ate weird things like bread so sour that it made my lips pucker. She said it was that way intentionally and I didn't believe her. She was obsessed with the human body, constantly amazed by it. She once called me into the bathroom to see her enormous poop and how it snaked around the bowl three times. "I did that!" she cried, proud. "Isn't that amazing?" It sorta was.

But they were on the outside because I met Paul. He was from Detroit. He would be my Ken, but a tougher Ken. A Ken raised in an all-black neighborhood in the heart of Detroit, even though he was white and Italian and Catholic. He was a genius and I loved his family and he made me feel like the world was safe and comfortable as long as I was near him. I ditched hanging out with my girlfriends so we could drive around in his Iroc Camaro, windows rolled down, Guns N' Roses blaring, singing at the top of our lungs, even though I thought the band sucked. I liked jazz, but you can't sound angry while singing to jazz.

When we broke up, I moved in with three women who would transform me: Kim, the artist; Rachel, the singer and attorney; Sarah, the director. We wore red lipstick. We ate pot roast. We talked about heart break. When Paul came over asking for me to come back to him, they supported me silently but blared "I'm a Creep" through their rooms. Sarah directed a play I wrote and Rachel starred in it and Kim helped with the posters. The friendship I had with Sarah was intense and confusing. We fought over the play. I told her I was embarrassed and wanted to know how she was directing it. She thought I didn't trust her, that I thought her work was crap. Really, I didn't trust myself. I was embarrassed by my words. I wasn't good enough. I dated an actor, and then I went back to Paul. Sarah dated someone out East, but still loved her high school sweetheart. I told her that you don't marry your high school sweetheart. That's what our mothers did. But what did I know? I didn't know anything. In the end, she married him, proving how wrong I was. About everything.

Paul and I moved to Miami so he could go to grad school and I could be a waitress. I met women who wanted more than life offered them. In the Beverly Hills Café, there were women who wanted to act, be a stewardess, find love. Women, like Gina, who was warm and from Georgia and had a laugh that could melt butter. I should've spent more time with them, but I was always with Paul. I should've asked them more questions. I should've been more present. Instead, I was always looking out the window, wondering how my boyfriend was.

I left Paul abruptly. Overnight, really. I said goodbye to him and it felt cruel. I did not get to say goodbye to his Italian mother. I missed her pragmatism. Her strength. The way she'd push the grocery cart in Kroger as if she was ready to run anyone down. She taught me the secret to her family's Italian pasta sauce, and I still feel guilty. I have never cooked it. I did not get to say goodbye to Paul's sister, Beth. We laughed together, curled up on the couch, eating Ben & Jerry's from little Dixie cups. We watched Anne of Green Gables over and over, though we were in college. I had red hair and she had brown hair and secretly, I pretended I was Anne and she was Diana and Paul was Gilbert and we would all live happily ever together. We did not.

On my own, in Grand Rapids, Michigan, I began to do theater. Community shows where I was in Assassins, and played Squeaky Fromme. I was in Angels in America, and I played Harper and I felt like I knew her because she was just as lost as I was. I became friends with Shelly and Tracey. We were called the Triumvirate, and I didn't know what that meant though I thought it was religious. We had big boobs. We laughed a lot. We drank more. At night, we'd meet up at the Cottage Bar & Grill, and we would pass around lemon drops. We'd flirt with men. We'd flirt with each other. We told secrets. We kept secrets. The friendships felt intense and like we would never be without each other. Then I moved to New York, and the friendships could not come with me.

There were others. Of course there were. Dionne and Ann and Vicki and Keeley and Arnie and Jeannie and Shayne and Amy. Women I envied for their beauty and their strength, for their intellect and creativity. Women I could've learned more from, and grown up with, and cared for. But I was jealous of them and angry. And petty. They were women that I put second and third and fourth because what was important wasn't friendships, but finding a man, getting married, having kids before my womb dried up at thirty.

I found a man. I had kids. I said goodbye to all my friends. Not consciously, but they slowly fell away, like leaves dropping. And now that I'm over forty, and remarried, and my kids are past the stage of needing me for every moment, it's not the 'wild years' of my twenties that I look back at with longing. It's all the women that have fluttered into my life. How they changed me. How they influenced me. And how I was never brave enough to hold on to them, to put friendship before dating, to give them the time and energy they deserve.

I wish I could have them back. All of them. The girlfriends that I have managed to keep over the years, I wish that we could be closer; but at least I get to see them occasionally for cocktails and stupid conversations. I wish I had a Sisterhood or something that wrapped in my old life and friendships with my new. We'd have potlucks, maybe. Book clubs. Something.

But it's hard to manage.

It's hard to reach out.

I wish I had my sister back.

I wish it was summer and we could sneak out of our houses, not to meet boys again...but to hang out under the stars and the moon. To look for fireflies. To laugh at each other. To say "Does this make me look fat?" and have the other say "God yes, but who the fuck cares?"

I wonder what they're doing now, these women I have loved and lost. All of them. I wonder, are they happy? Do they laugh? Do they ever think of me? And if they do, I hope it's with fondness. I hope it's with understanding.

Main Dishes

What separates a Main Dish from a lunch or even an appetizer? This is a serious question and I have spent many an hour contemplating it.

See, there I am sitting at a coffee table looking extremely intellectual and I'm thinking "What makes a Main Dish main?"

Or I'm at the grocery store, rubbing my chin, contemplatively thinking, "Hmmmmmm".

Or I'm staring into the great blue yonder wondering what is the philosophical difference between lunch and dinner…or *mind explosion*…dinner and supper?

It doesn't matter. The only thing I can come up with is Quantity. So, if you eat more of something, it's probably a main dish. Or not.

Really, who the fuck cares? In fact, why am I separating these recipes at all? Such a dumb ass idea. There's no difference what a dish is. If you eat that food for breakfast, then that's breakfast food. It feels good kinda having this ultimate power over the naming of things. Dessert: a baked potato with sour cream and chives and butter. Main dish: seven chocolate chip cookies.

Here are some main dishes for you that make more servings than a plate of olive cheese balls. But if you want to make a plate of olive cheese balls your main meal, you'll get no judgment from me.

Broccoli (Chicken) Rice Casserole

When You Want Comfort Food
But Don't Actually Need Comfort

I was raised in the Midwest (Michigan to be exact) and I'm not sure what our cultural cuisine is, but I'd probably argue it's a casserole.

My mom was a single mom trying to make it on her own in the seventies and eighties. Sometimes she'd have a sudden inspiration and cook eggrolls or artichokes for us, but mostly it was TV dinners, chipped beef on toast, or a rice casserole. My favorite was chicken and rice. Basically, cream of mushroom soup, rice, and a chicken breast on top, all cooked together. If you're thinking "Man, that does not sound like there's any flavor in there" you're right. It was comforting though, and I added a lot of salt.

Also, sometimes my mom would take me to these folk dancing get-togethers. It was Potluck City. Everyone was hairy and there was a lot of macramé and carob chips. And then people stood in a circle, held hands and then started spinning and rotating and stuff to lutes or something. Northern Michigan in the 70s. Living the good life.

This next recipe is free from carob chips and hair, thankfully.

It's broccoli rice casserole and it hits all my spots for when my mood is just fine, but I'm feeling nostalgic for record players, corduroy, and rotary phones. There is flavor, but it's muted Midwest flavor. The kind of flavor that says "Hi" and "I'm sorry".

It's old school. It's simple. If your tummy doesn't feel great or you have a cold, this is perfect food. Also, it heats up great. I've been known to have this for breakfast.

And lunch.

And snacks.

So, basically, I just eat it around the clock.

Stuff You Need

2 cups rice (cooked. Leftover rice works fine.)

2 1/2–3 cups chicken (cooked and shredded, or chopped. I use rotisserie chicken. If you want a vegetarian casserole, omit chicken and add some more veggies.)

2 cups broccoli (bite size or chopped. Frozen works fine. Defrosted. If using fresh, parboil for a few minutes.)

10 oz can condensed cream of chicken soup

1 cup sour cream

1/2 cup milk

1-1/2 cups cheddar cheese (shredded)

1 tsp salt

2 cups crushed, round, buttery crackers (like Ritz.)

4 tbsp butter (melted)

What You Do

1. Preheat the oven to 350°.
2. In a large bowl, stir together rice, chicken, broccoli, cream of chicken soup, sour cream, milk, cheese, and salt
3. Spray a 9x13 with cooking spray and pour mixture in.
4. Mix together crushed round crackers and melted butter in a small bowl.
5. Sprinkle crushed crackers evenly over the top of the casserole.
6. Bake for 25 minutes, or until it's bubbly and smells good.

White Chicken Chili

When You Want Nourishment & Warmth

Stuff You Need

1 to 2 cups chicken breasts, cooked, cut into bite-sized pieces (Just use a rotisserie chicken)
1 cup chopped onion
2 garlic cloves, minced
1 tsp ground cumin
1/4 tsp dry oregano
1/2 tsp ground coriander
1 - 4.5 oz can chopped green chilies, un-drained
1 - 15.5 oz can of cannellini beans, rinsed and drained
2 cans chicken broth (use more if desired)

Toppings (optional)
Cheese
Parsley
Green onions
Sour cream

What You Do

1. Heat onions and cook until translucent; about five minutes.
2. Add garlic, cook an additional minute.
3. Add chicken and spices and heat until fragrant.
4. Add chilies, beans, and as much chicken broth until you reach desired consistency.
5. Simmer on stove until flavors meld. I also like to add in some sour cream (about 1/4 cup) before serving to make it creamy.

You can also just dump all of this in a crockpot and cook it for a few hours.

WHAT LOVE FEELS LIKE
Warm, comforting hands
holding onto me
so that i don;t
float away

Grilled Shrimp Foil Packets

When You Want Someone Else To Do The Cooking

It's not that I can't use the grill. I just don't know how to turn it on.

Once it's on, I'm pretty sure I can cook on there.

Sometimes, I just don't want to cook. Sometimes I just want to sit and fan myself and have someone else cook while I take random naps. This happens a lot in July when it's humid as fuck. But it also happens on Any Day At All. Sometimes I just don't want to do anything.

Maybe you can relate.

In the summer, or really any time, my husband will make this. Basically, you mix everything in a bowl and then divvy it up into tinfoil packets. Sometimes I help. Sometimes I retreat to the fainting couch while I have the vapors. Or whatever. I make something up so I can get out of helping. Then he does it and pops it on the grill.

I have to say, there's something fun about getting your meal to you in a foil packet. Maybe for me because it brings up memories of Jiffy Pop about to explode on the stove, and I just watch as every pop made that silver bag inflate a little more. There was a certain suspense to it: watching it slowly inflate and wondering if the next pop would be just too much and the whole thing would explode.

Not that these foil packets will explode. They won't. Because exploding shrimp and projectile corncobs might sound fun, but would really be a nightmare.

Maybe I like this recipe because it feels like a TV Dinner to me, and that always excites me. Or maybe, just maybe, I like this recipe because it's freaking GOOD.

This works great to serve to a crowd because you can make so much of it.

When you open the foil packet (after you've put it in a bowl), you'll get this burst of fragrance: Lemon, Old Bay Seasoning spice, a hint of shrimp, and that lovely buttery scent of cooked corn and potatoes.

Serve this with biscuits or some kind of bread to sop up the juices.

You will want to sop.

Stuff You Need

1-1/2 lb. large shrimp, peeled and deveined. We usually use defrosted, but I bet you could keep them frozen and it'd still work.

2 cloves garlic, minced

2 smoked sausages or kielbasa, sliced in ½ inch pieces.

2 ears corn, each cut into 4 pieces each

1 lb. red bliss potatoes, chopped into 1-inch pieces

2 tbsp extra-virgin olive oil

1 tbsp Old Bay seasoning

Kosher salt

Freshly ground black pepper

2 tbsp freshly chopped parsley

1 lemon, sliced into thin wedges

4 tbsp Butter

If you want to eat more, then double the recipe.

What You Do

1. Preheat grill over high heat, or preheat oven to 425°. Cut 4 sheets of foil about 16 inches long. In a big ol' bowl add shrimp, garlic, sausage, corn, and potatoes. Drizzle with oil, then add Old Bay seasoning and season to taste with salt and pepper. Toss gently to combine. Divvy up on the foil sheets. Top each mixture with parsley, lemon and a tablespoon of butter each.

2. Fold foil packets over the shrimp boil mixture to completely cover the food. Roll top and bottom edges to seal them closed. You're making, basically, an envelope of food that you will open later. It's very exciting.

3. Place foil packets on grill and cook until just cooked through, about 15 to 20 minutes (or transfer to oven and bake for 20 minutes).

Instant Pot Butter Chicken

When You Want Indian Takeout
But You Don't Want To Drive Or Walk Anywhere

Stuff You Need

1 14-ounce canned tomatoes

6 cloves garlic (yep. It's garlic-licious)

1 tsp minced ginger (frozen ginger works great)

1 tsp Turmeric

1/4 tsp Cayenne (if you like spice, add more. I'm afraid of spice. Too much flavor.)

1 tsp Smoked Paprika

1 tsp Salt

1 tsp Garam Masala (this is a fragrant spice and you really shouldn't skip it.)

1 tsp Ground Cumin

1 pound boneless, skinless chicken thighs. (You can use chicken breasts, but breast meat gets a little dry and chewy.)

FOR THE SAUCE

4 ounces butter cut into cubes (This is why it's called Butter Chicken! Because BUTTER.)

4 ounces heavy cream

1 tsp Garam Masala

Chopped cilantro (optional. Cilantro tastes like soap to me so I use chopped parsley.)

What You Do

1. Place all ingredients into an Instant Pot in the order listed, EXCEPT for the ingredients for the sauce. Hold onto those.
2. Mix the ingredients (except for the sauce stuff) well and then top with the chicken. If you just mixed everything together, that's fine too.
3. Seal. Cook on high pressure for 10 minutes, then let it slow release for 10 minutes. Release all pressure before opening or KABOOM! (I'm not sure that there would really be a KABOOM, but better to be cautious.)
4. Remove chicken with slotted spoon and set aside.
5. Make the sauce! This is what you have been waiting for! You have also been waiting for a cottage by the lake to be magically gifted to you, but you'll have to keep waiting for that. But THE SAUCE, you can make now. Blend together all the ingredients in the pot using, using an immersion blender. Don't have an immersion blender? Get creative! Mash it with a fork or stir really hard or just say "Fuck it. It's still a sauce, with or without a fucking Immersion Blender.)
6. Let the sauce cool a smidge, then add in your butter, cream and chopped cilantro or parsley. Stir.
7. Add the chicken back to the pot. I like to chop it into bite size pieces.
8. Serve over rice.

If you have a ton of sauce left over, you can add peas and paneer to it for a new dish! Or freeze it and add rotisserie chicken to it later when you want food but don't want to cook. Just microwave that shit, and you've got dinner again.

I'm telling you, this recipe is amazing. It's easy, cooks a ton, and is delicious re-heated. I serve this with naan. If you want to make a feast, try cooking up dome samosas and dal. Rice is a must with this.

I don't have a lot more to say here, mostly because I want to take a nap.

Polenta Fries And Bruschetta

When You Want The Ultimate Vegetarian Meal And You Also Want To Be Cocky About It

Somewhere in this cookbook, I talk about polenta. How to make it. How it's amazing. And then how to make it into fries. So, do all that. I love to make polenta fries the day after I've had regular polenta. And this duo makes a really nice lunch.

And, god, it's good.

It's really pretty too.

It's, as they say, Instagrammable.

This is the ultimate appetizer because it's super flavorful, healthy, pretty, and easy. There are not really measurements here because it all depends on the juiciest of your tomatoes. And how much garlic you like. And if the moon is waxing or waning. Just taste test! Pretend you're a master chef and you don't need no damn recipe. But here's the recipe anyway. Sorta.

I should probably tell you how I learned this recipe. I went to a cottage with a guy friend. Because I love cottages. I didn't love the guy. He was nice. I liked him. He was a friend. What I envisioned as a cool couple of days by the beach, he envisioned as a romantic getaway for two with some horizontal fornication.

I had my period and it was terrible; and I had cramps like I was giving birth to Cthulhu. So, I told him that.

It might've been too much information. He made me a fancy dinner anyway, which included this recipe. We stayed in the friend zone and then he kind of faded into the ether, along with my cramps.

The recipe remains.

Stuff You Need

FOR THE BRUSCHETTA

Chopped fresh tomatoes (heirlooms are great if in season, but you can also make this with regular store tomatoes)

Diced garlic (start with one clove and move up from there.)
Olive oil
Salt
French baguette
Basil
Parmesan

What You Do

1. Preheat oven to 425°. Slice your baguette on the diagonal so you have nice little toasts. Put them on a cookie sheet. Drizzle with olive oil and bake for about 5 minutes or until golden brown. Set aside to cool.
2. In a bowl, add your chopped tomatoes and garlic. Sprinkle with salt. Drizzle with olive oil. Taste it. Is it too garlicky? Not garlicky enough? Did you add enough salt? There should be some juice here, so add enough olive oil that there's a little tomato juiciness in the bottom of the bowl. Let it sit for a bit.
3. To serve: take your baguette and spoon a mound of bruschetta onto it. Top with a little shredded basil and parmesan. Serve and eat.
4. Serve with your polenta fries for a beautiful little dish. If you need a protein, add a protein! Grilled chicken goes great with it.

POLENTA FRIES

Preheat oven to 450°. Dump your firm polenta onto a cutting board. Poke it. It kinda jiggles. It's kinda kinky, this polenta. Now focus. Slice the polenta into fry shapes. Or bug shapes. Or hearts. Whatever. Place on a parchment covered cookie sheet. Drizzle liberally with olive oil. Sprinkle with sea salt. Cook until crunchy, flipping about half way through. It'll take 30 to 45 minutes. It's a long time, but worth the wait.

Sesame Chicken

When You Want Your Kids To Just Eat Already

I may sound like I complain a lot in this book. That's because I complain a lot in this book. I guess it's genetic because my kids also complain a lot. Especially when everyone is hungry.

Hangry…that's a real thing people.

This is a family-friendly recipe. You don't have to have kids at all to make it or eat it. It's just a go-to in my house when everyone is hungry, and we don't know what to eat or one or all of us are grumpy. We usually have all the ingredients on hand. Serve with rice and edamame. You can also cook up some ramen noodles and serve it with that. I usually jazz up the ramen, but you can decide if you feel like being jazzy or not.

YUM!

Stuff You Need

- 1 cup panko (Japanese) breadcrumbs
- 2 tbsp sesame seeds
- 1/2 tsp salt
- 1 pound chicken breast tenders (or you can slice chicken breasts, or cut them into chunks)
- 1 large egg, lightly beaten

SAUCE (Optional):
- 2 garlic cloves, minced
- 1 tbsp minced peeled fresh ginger
- 1/4 cup low-sodium soy sauce
- 3 tbsp rice vinegar
- 4 tsps honey
- 1/4 cup chopped scallions

What You Do

1. Combine the panko, sesame seeds, and salt in a shallow plate. I like to use a pie plate because it's easier.
2. Dip the chicken breast tenders into the egg. Then dredge the chicken breast tenders in the panko–sesame seed mixture.
3. Heat 2 tbsp or so of vegetable oil in a large nonstick skillet over medium-high heat. Add the chicken breast tenders and cook 4–5 minutes per side, or until cooked through. Wipe out the pan.
4. If the tenders are big, or you don't want to totally pan-cook them, you can cook on each side until golden and transfer them to a cookie sheet. Once you've browned everything, cook in the oven at 425° for about 10 minutes.
5. Cook your rice or ramen and edamame.
6. Serve with soy sauce…or here's a quick sauce that's really yummy.
7. In a small saucepan, add a little vegetable or sesame oil and cook minced garlic and fresh ginger for about one minute, or until soft. Remove from heat and stir in the soy sauce, rice vinegar, and honey.

Plate it up and eat! I use little plastic ramekins for the sauce and the kids either dip their sesame chicken in it or pour a little sauce over the rice.

How to Make me Love you

wrap your fingers in my hair

kiss the side of my neck

write me a letter in pen
play a song for me

kiss me in the sunlight
while others watch

tell me the truth

Tell me we're strong enough
to handle it

"I Want You To Fuck Me Before Dinner" Pasta

When You Want Romance And Food In Your Life

I'm going to share this secret with you at the risk of TMI. Here's the thing. When you make pasta with someone, it's so freaking romantic, you'll probably skip the pasta and just have amazing sex while you're both lightly dusted with flour.

That's one of the main reasons I make pasta! The sex!

Also, okay, because it's amazing. Like, A M A Z I N G.

It's hard to write about how to make pasta. You should probably watch a YouTube video on it. But the method, I can share with you. Basically, you make the dough. I usually use my food processor, but you can use your hands if you just want to get in there. The making of the dough isn't necessarily sexy, unless your loved one pours you a glass of wine and starts feeding you shrimp and kissing the side of your neck. Then. Okay. This is sexy.

So, you make the dough, and then you let it rest for an hour.

What will you and your loved one do while the dough rests?

WHAT WILL YOU DO?

Are you seriously asking me that question? By this time, you've had a glass of wine, you've made dough, and you're feeling damned proud of yourself. So proud, your nipples are probably pert. I don't care if you're male or female. Those nipples are standing up and saying OH HI! OVER HERE!

So, for the next hour, listen to your nipples. Grab your partner and spend the next hour nibbling each other.

Then when your pasta is rested and you have post-coital endorphins happening, return to the pasta. You cut the ball of dough into about six pieces, covering each with plastic wrap. Then you flatten one of the pieces, dust it with flour, and start threading it through your pasta maker, each time getting that little dough a little bit thinner and longer.

This is where things get hot in the kitchen.

Have your second glass of wine. Put on some Sexy Time music. Now, have your partner help you. That pasta is going to get long and unwieldy and both of you will need your hands and elbows and arms up in there. It's very much like the pottery wheel scene in Ghost, but this time, your partner is 100% alive. You can tell they're alive because they're so turned on that after a few minutes of kneading the dough, they start kneading YOU. If you've never been kneaded, it's great. It develops all your gluten.

Sprinkle your noodles with flour and put them on a cookie sheet to dry, or put the cookie sheet in the freezer.

Then go have sex again. Because you'll want to.

By the time you're done, you'll have worked up an appetite. What are you going to make for dinner?

Oh! That's right! Pasta!

Boil your water and add enough salt so it tastes sea-like without the funk. Cook your pasta for about 3 minutes. Toss with butter, salt, pepper and a little Parmesan, and then eat it.

Eat from one bowl with your loved one, taking turns.

You will leave this meal feeling satiated. And loved.

If you make this pasta alone, you can still get turned on. Just take breaks to love yourself. It's just as good.

Homemade Pasta

With Whatever Kind Of Sauce You Want (If You Can Even Make It To The Point Where You Put Sauce On It)

Stuff You Need

- 2 ½ cups flour (plus more for dusting)
- 3 eggs
- 1 tbsp olive oil
- 1 tsp salt

What You Do

1. Put flour and salt in food processor. Pulse a couple of times to combine. Add the oil and one egg. Give it a 30 second pulse.
2. Add another egg and pulse. (Look at all the pulsing!) Add the last egg and continue to mix until it all comes together. Give it a little time. If it seems dry or isn't coming together, add a little water.
3. Turn onto a floured surface and make it into a ball. Cover with an inverted bowl or wrap in plastic wrap and let rest for 30 minutes. You can also refrigerate it, then bring it to room temperature when you're ready to make your pasta.
4. Next, make your pasta. Watch a video, because it will take me forever to explain what to do here, and you'll just end up watching a video anyway.
5. I love fresh pasta with shrimp scampi, or simply pesto and sundried tomatoes. My favorite ravioli is stuffed with goat cheese and lemon zest and tossed with garlic butter and parsley.

Veggie Rice Breakfast Casserole

When You Want To Feel Like You're Well Balanced And Eating Healthy

Sometimes I want my favorite breakfast: 2 over-medium eggs, hash browns, bacon, and rye toast. When I want that, I go to a restaurant and ask for that. They magically bring it to me, but only because I give them money.

When I'm at home, my breakfasts are simpler, because I'm tired and/or I don't have time. Rice cake with peanut butter, banana, and honey. Leftovers from the night before. Sausage links eaten standing up by the kitchen sink while I make my kids their breakfast and try to navigate their teenage moodiness.

But sometimes I cook up this rice dish and keep in the fridge for a quick breakfast. It's super easy, inspired by the Moosewood recipe, and you can add endless things to it to vary it. I like mine with pan fried zucchini, mushrooms, and tomatoes. They add soy sauce and a ton of rice to their recipe, but I don't do that. Because it's MY recipe.

This is a meal that feels good to eat. It also makes me want to dress in a peasant skirt and a tank top, go make up free, and maybe stop shaving my armpits. This is not a put down. I REPEAT: NOT A PUT DOWN. Because when I eat this, I feel good about myself and I don't need anything extra. Not even deodorant.

Stuff You Need

- 2 cups cooked basmati rice (or brown rice or whatever)
- 2 tbsp olive oil
- 1 medium onion, diced
- 8 oz cremini or white mushrooms, chopped
- 2 cloves garlic, minced
- 2 man-handfuls baby spinach, chopped
- 1 tsp kosher or sea salt
- 3 eggs, beaten
- 1/2 cup milk
- 1 cup grated cheddar or mozzarella cheese
- 1/3 cup sunflower seeds (optional, but I like the crunch)

What You Do

1. Preheat oven to 375°.
2. Spray a 9x13 baking dish or casserole with cooking spray and set aside.
3. Cook the rice and set aside. Or better yet, just use leftover rice, or that frozen rice from Trader Joe's that takes 3 minutes to cook.
4. Heat olive oil in a large stockpot over medium heat. Add onions and mushrooms and sauté until everything is soft and a little golden. Add in garlic and other vegetables if you want, or stick to 2 handfuls of spinach. This morning I used one cup of leftover roasted vegetables (cauliflower, broccoli, carrots and brussels sprouts) and it was delicious. You can also add in cooked sausage or ham if you want some extra protein.
5. Let cool for a few minutes, then add rice, eggs, milk, cheese and stir to combine.
6. Spread evenly in baking dish. Top with sunflower seeds. Cover with tinfoil and bake for 25 minutes, then remove foil and bake uncovered for another 10 minutes. But it might take longer, depending on how much rice and veggies you have. You want it to bounce back when you tap on it. Eggs should be cooked.

Tamale Pie

When You Just Want To Eat A Shit Ton Of Casserole

Oh god. I love Tamale Pie. I love it I love it I love it. There's a tamale pie that's made with Doritos and sour cream and I have to tell you, that was maybe the first time I had an orgasm. I ate it, orgasmed and then asked dad what had just happened to me. It was a mortifying experience and I don't recommend asking your dad to explain an orgasm to you.

But then over the years, my tastes changed a bit.

No, they didn't. That's a fucking lie. I still love the Dorito version, but I can't get anyone in my household to eat it.

This pie is, I guess, more sophisticated because it has natural ingredients, like Jiffy cornbread mix.

Make this. Eat it. Eat it now, and eat it later, because it's great heated up. Have it with Doritos if you want to, or an avocado drizzled with sea salt and olive oil. Who cares? You be you. That's what's important.

Also, this tamale pie is important.

And easy.

So…yay.

Stuff You Need

- 1 box cornbread mix
- 1 small can corn
- 1 can kidney or pinto beans
- 1 onion, chopped
- 1 pound ground beef
- 1 package taco seasoning
- 3/4 cup water
- Sour cream
- Shredded cheddar

What You Do

1. In a large skillet, add onions and ground beef, then cook until browned. Drain. Add taco seasoning mix and ¾ cup water, and simmer for ten minutes or until most of the sauce has cooked off. Mix drained beans and corn with meat mixture and pour into casserole dish.
2. Spread a layer of sour cream over mixture and top generously with shredded cheddar.
3. Mix corn bread according to package and then spread over top of the meat mixture.
4. Bake at 400° for a half an hour or until the cornbread begins to brown.
5. Serve with salsa and sour cream.

Interlude

For some reason, I just remembered the time my stepsister, Heidi, tried to teach me about blow jobs. We were on one of our many walks around Coopersville. She was 16, I was 15. She was a pom pom girl and popular and pretty and had hair so huge that I'm pretty sure she pissed off some Gods. They didn't know that the secret was Aqua Net. And a lot of it.

At 15, I was nonsexual, moody, fancied myself a poet, and looked like the lead singer from Simply Red. The last thing on my mind was how to give a blow job.

We stopped at the local QuickStop downtown and picked up Rocket Pops, our favorite popsicles. Blueberry, lemon and raspberry flavor, cold and so good.

"Tanya," she said, "You need to learn how to give a blow job."

"Why?" I asked. I really wanted to know.

"Because some day you're going to have to give one to your boyfriend or your husband. Unless you're a lesbian, then you won't have to worry about it. Are you a lesbian?"

"I'm not anything," I said. And I wasn't. (I wouldn't be anything until two years later when I was a senior and a mysterious boy named Will moved to town. He smelled like musty sweaters and I loved him with all my heart. And part of my ovaries.)

We stopped by the baseball field so she could show me how to lick and deep throat the rocket pop.

"See?" she said. "Easy. Now it's your turn."

I smiled and took a very satisfying, aggressive BITE out of my Rocket Pop.

"Lesbian," she said and nodded.

Mojo Pork
(To Get Your Mojo Back)

When You Feel Meh

Slow cookers!!

Now, I know a lot of these recipes seem a little sad. Like, here's something to eat when you're clinically depressed! But that's not my intention. My intention is…

Fuck. I don't know.

I guess I am sad a lot. Or not sad, really, but introspective. Moody.

Emotionally needy and maladjusted. Melancholic. Feeling a deep sense of ennui.

Whatever.

But this recipe isn't for when you're blue. Though it CAN be. It's for when you just need a little, I don't know, OOMPH. Sometimes, your energy level gets low in life, or love, or when you're playing video games and you've run out of your fighting force. Or you have anemia.

This will give you your life force back.

Or, if it doesn't give you your life force back, it will at least give you a delicious few meals of burritos, tacos, bowls, nachos, etc. Also, this makes an amazing topping for Tamale Pie, or in your Cuban sandwich. Holy shit. So good.

Another benefit, you do a little bit of prep and then toss it in the slow cooker and let it cook all day so you can do other important things. Like nap. (Although tossing a 4 pound hunk of meat can be challenging.)

Stuff You Need

2 tbs vegetable or canola oil
2 tsp Kosher salt
1/4 tsp black pepper
4 pound pork shoulder
1/4 cup orange juice
1/4 cup lime juice
2 tsp cumin
2 tsp dried oregano

1/4 tsp crushed red pepper flakes
  (optional)
4 cloves garlic minced
2 leaves bay

What You Do

1. In a large pot add the vegetable or canola oil on medium high heat.
2. Season the pork with the kosher salt and black pepper and brown the pork on all sides. This might not seem like an important step, and you may not want to do it, but try. Because if you skip it, then your meat is going to be all gray. And All gray meat is about as appealing as a loaf of firm uncooked tofu. So, brown this on all sides. It's the most work you'll have to do the whole day, and you'll be glad you did it.
3. To the slow cooker add the orange juice, lime juice, cumin, oregano, red pepper flakes, garlic, and bay leaves Mix it together.
4. Add the pork to the slow cooker and roll it in the mixture until it is coated well.
5. Cook on low for 8 hours or on high for 6.
6. When the pork is done you can serve as-is with the juice on top. Shred it and remove the excess fat. Save some for now but freeze some with the juice for later.

What To Do Now That I Have Some Mojo?

Here are some options:

Cook up some rice using coconut milk in place of water. Make yourself a rice bowl with rice, mojo pork, corn, peppers or spinach, and a side of plantains.

It's a great filling for tacos. Get corn tortillas. Add a little lime *crema*. So good!

Stuff a burrito. To make a wet burrito, you can do a Michigan Wet Burrito sauce. Okay. This is my burrito sauce: 1 cup brown gravy, 1 cup enchilada sauce. Pour over your burrito, top with cheddar cheese, and cook 10-15 minutes in 425° oven until cheese is bubbly.

Or you can use mojo pork to top Tamale Pie, instead of using ground beef.

Old School Meatloaf With Mashed Potatoes And Roasted Green Beans

When You Want Old School American Cooking

What You Do

Buy a pack of Lipton Beef & Onion Instant Soup Mix and follow the recipe on the back of the box. Bam! Done.

Then if you want MORE comfort, make mashed potatoes in your Instant Pot.

Peel some potatoes. Golden potatoes are the best. Chop them into equal size chunks. You don't have to be perfect with this. What size chunks? Doesn't matter really, but somewhere between the size of a fat grape or a ping pong ball.

Put a metal steamer or colander in your Instant pot. Add 1 cup of water. Add your potatoes. Sprinkle with salt.

Seal. Steam for 10 minutes. Quick release.

Mash your potatoes with a masher, your bare hands (hot though) or a hand mixer. Add a SHIT TON of butter and a dab of milk. If you want to be extra fancy, add in some sour cream or cheddar cheese. Heck, add in sour cream AND cheddar cheese AND chives AND bacon. Now you have Loaded Mashed Potatoes and you have reached Comfort Nirvana.

You probably should have something green with this meal because life is about balance, motherfucker.

ROASTED GREEN BEANS

When your meatloaf is done and resting, crank your oven to 450°. Put green beans on a tin foil lined sheet, drizzle with olive oil and sprinkle with sea salt. Roast until the beans start to sizzle and pop and get a little brown. About 5 minutes or so.

This is a meal that your family will love and thank you for being so old-school and epic.

Recipe For Whatever

When You've Been Working Really Really Hard And You Barely Have Enough Energy To Watch Netflix

Oh, honey! If this is how you're feeling, don't even think about cooking!! Order Door Dash or something. Grab those take out menus. Have a world buffet where you order from three different places. Eating totally alone? WHO THE FUCK CARES? Leftovers make the world go around.

Place your hand on your heart and your belly.

Close your eyes.

Now, ask yourself "What do I really need right now? What will both soothe me and nourish me?"

Listen to the quiet voice inside you. Maybe it's a husky whisper of "currrrrrrrry" or maybe it's RA-MEN and SUSHI. Or maybe it's a trill of the word ENORMOUS BURRITO.

If you're tired and all you want to do is eat takeout and watch TV, do that thing.

You can always cook tomorrow.

Or not.

What You Do

If you don't have energy to make anything, don't make anything. Indulge. Call takeout. Call a friend to come over. Order pizza. Or eat that sad frozen dinner that's been in your freezer for ever. The one you bought for a dire emergency. This is that emergency. Eat that fucking terrible meal. Or let your meal be a bag of microwave popcorn and some red wine. It doesn't matter. Eat something, because food is energy and you need energy right now. Just get through the night. Stream something mindless. Or just go to bed. Sleep. Let your body heal from the inside out. Rest. Give yourself permission to be in pain, and then give yourself permission to step out of the pain long enough to go to the grocery store and get some easy things to make for yourself. Maybe it's something small and ridiculously easy. A loaf of bread. Peanut butter. Jam.

Feed your body, and in time you will feed your soul.

Side Dishes

I have to admit. I don't really understand the concept of side dishes. I guess they're called side dishes because they're supposed to accompany whatever enormous protein you've put on your plate. But what if you want more side dishes and only a tiny bit of protein? Who's the side dish now, bitch?

Anyway...

Here are some things you can eat on the side, or eat as the main highlight. You can eat a little or a lot. You're in control here.

You have the power.

Polenta

When You Want A Side Dish That Is Also An Appetizer And A Main Dish

I love polenta. I can't explain why, but there's just something so simple and delicious about it. Polenta is luscious and creamy and thick, but when it's chilled, it's firm and you can slice, but then when you fry it, it gets crisp on the outside, but the inside reverts back to being smooth and creamy and luscious. It's some kind of mobius strip of food. That doesn't sound very appetizing, but it is. Mobius strips are delicious.

Plus, you can make fries out of this.

Stuff You Need

6-2/3 cups chicken broth (use bone broth for extra awesome)

2 tsp each of marjoram, thyme, and sage (Optional. Good without too.)

1 garlic clove, crushed.

1-2/3 cup yellow cornmeal or polenta

2 Tbs butter

1 cup cheese (mozzarella or combine mozzarella and parmesan)

What You Do

1. Combine and bring to a boil: chicken broth, herbs, and garlic.
2. Whisk in slowly 1-2/3 cup yellow cornmeal or polenta
3. Reduce heat to barely simmering. Stir continuously until spoon stands up in bowl and polenta pulls away from side: about 30 minutes*. Yes. 30 minutes.
4. When polenta is cooked, remove from heat and add 1 cup mozzarella or parmesan. Serve immediately or pour and spread polenta into a greased pan and cool.

*If you don't want to wait 30 minutes, you can also buy instant polenta. It cooks in three minutes and is terrific. But old school style is a little tastier. Plus, if you make it old-school style, you get to tell everyone how much effort you went through to make their meal.

Uses

- Serve with roasted chicken, grilled steak, or shrimp.
- You can top it with roasted cherry tomatoes and goat cheese, or sautéed mushrooms.
- Top it with marinara or meat sauce for a spin on spaghetti.
- If you have extra polenta, spray a glass pan with nonstick spray and the pour polenta in it. Refrigerate until firm. Why? Because then you can make…

Breaded polenta!

Polenta Fries

What You Do

1. Heat oven to 425°.
2. Line a cookie sheet with parchment.
3. Slice your chilled polenta into fries and drizzle liberally with olive oil. Sprinkle with sea salt.
4. Cook for 30 to 45 minutes. For real. It takes a long time to crisp these up and you want them crisp. When you hold up the fry, it should stand tall and proud, and not all impotent and wilted.
5. When golden and crisp, serve and eat.

Great with sandwiches, soup, bruschetta, or just on its own.

Polenta Stuffed With Goat Cheese And Sun-Dried Tomatoes

Stuff You Need

2 eggs, beaten
1 cup seasoned breadcrumbs
6 oz goat cheese (I like Boursin)
1/4 cup sun dried tomatoes in oil, drained and chopped
1 14 oz. can diced tomatoes
Use chilled, firm polenta for this.

What You Do

1. Preheat oven to 450°. Spray cookie sheet with cooking spray. Set aside. Cut polenta into 1 ½ inch slices. Dip polenta slice in egg, then in breadcrumbs until slice is coated. Place on cookie sheet and bake until golden brown, about 30-40 minutes, turning over once.
2. When polenta is cooked, remove from oven. Slice each polenta piece in the center (careful not to cut through entirely) and stuff with 1 tablespoon goat cheese and sun-dried tomatoes. The goat cheese will melt from the heat of the polenta.
3. Heat tomatoes until warmed.

On a serving plate, serve 2 slices of stuffed polenta, topped with 1/3 cup tomatoes.

Rice Salad

When You Want A Salad But No Lettuce

I'm currently on a cruise to Key West and the Bahamas while I write this. The ship is vibrating, but not quite enough to cause any pleasure and there's the faint scent of exhaust in the air. It's okay though because we've found the one quiet place on the ship where there's no one who's drunk and shouting "WohoooOO!"

I've forgotten where I was going with this.

Oh, yes.

So, I sit down to write the recipe for RICE SALAD and my first thought is, "Rice Salad? What the fuck is that? Who wants a salad made from rice? What is wrong with you Tanya?"

I'm not sure what I was thinking. So now I have to search through my recipes and figure out what was going on with my mind when I wrote a note to myself to "Write about the Rice Salad".

Maybe there's more than a faint hint of exhaust in the air.

Hmmmm.

Stuff You Need

FOR THE SALAD

Cooked brown rice, about 1-1/2 cups
1/2 sliced green onion
1 stalk celery, sliced
1/4 red bell pepper, cubed
1 small carrot, grated
2 dried apricots, chopped finely
1/4 fennel bulb, diced
Sunflower seeds to taste.

FOR THE DRESSING

1/2 cup olive oil
Juice of 1/2 lemon
1 clove of garlic, peeled, left whole, and
    make an x at the end
1 tbsp tahini
1 tbsp maple syrup
1 tbsp soy sauce
1 tsp Dijon mustard
Salt and pepper

What You Do

1. Mix salad ingredients together in a big ol' bowl. Done.
2. For the dressing: Put all the ingredients for the dressing in a jar with a lid and shake. Voila. Done.
3. Mix the dressing and dress the salad to taste.

It'll make a lot of dressing. It's great on a regular kind of salad too, so just keep it on hand in the fridge.

Here's to your health. And to fennel. It's a vegetable worthy of more love.

Veggie Cheese Cascade

When You Want To Cook Like It's The 1970s And Macramé Is Still Popular

This recipe…this recipe makes me laugh and delights me at the same time. It makes me think of shag carpeting, macramé owl wall hangings and zipping around in corduroy pants. Maybe that's because I was born in 1973 and we'd eat this at every family get together.

It's kind of a weird recipe. It's basically veggies and cheese. That's it. But there's something really good about that, too. This is a good side dish, or you can eat it as a main dish. You'll want some bread with it and maybe a bowl of fruit drizzled with honey.

Loaded with gooey cheese, this side dish is rich, decadent, but you can justify it by saying it's got vegetables in it. Another thing that's easy to serve to a big group.

Stuff You Need

2 1-lb bags of mixed, frozen veggies (If you want a vintage 1970s feel)
OR
Mixed fresh veggies (broccoli, cauliflower, green beans, carrots or squash, Brussels sprouts.)
1 medium onion, chopped
6-8 ounces mozzarella, shredded
6-8 ounces Swiss, shredded
6-8 ounces cheddar, shredded
1 pint sour cream

What You Do

1. Cook veggies and onions until veggies are thawed and onion is soft; drain. If you're cooking fresh veggies, you might want to roast them in a 450° oven until tender.
2. When veggies are done, place them in greased casserole and mix with sour cream. Layer cheese on top.
3. Bake 1/2 hour at 325°. Stir after baking. Cheese will crust after 1/2 an hour.

Lentil Salad With Goat Cheese And Walnuts

When You Want Fancy Fiber

Fancy people call this a French Lentil Salad. I'm not sure why. Maybe because of the goat cheese. I just call it something I like to eat. Admittedly, it's good with a nice chunk of French Bread and a glass of cool white wine.

It is, actually, my lifelong quest to get everyone on my house to enjoy lentils as much as I do. And it's totally not working. Which is fine, because then when I make this salad, I have it all to myself. It's kind of selfish without actually being selfish, because no one really wants it anyway.

Incorporate this into your I'm Eating Healthy Now meal plan. And then later, have a pizza. Everyone likes pizza.

Stuff You Need

1-1/2 cups green lentils
1 bay leaf
3 sprigs thyme
1 carrot, peeled and finely diced
1 small red onion, peeled and
  finely diced
1 rib celery, finely diced

For the Dressing:
1 tablespoon red wine vinegar
1 1/4 tsps sea salt or kosher salt,
  plus more as needed

1 tsp Dijon mustard
1/3 cup olive oil, or half walnut oil
  and half olive oil
1 small shallot, peeled and minced
  (The shallot is EVERYTHING in
  this dressing. Don't leave it out!)
Freshly ground black pepper
1/2 cup finely chopped fresh flat-
  leaf parsley
1 cup walnuts or pecans, toasted
  and coarsely chopped
1 cup crumbled fresh or slightly
  aged goat cheese or feta cheese

What You Do

1. Rinse the lentils and pick out any freaks of nature. Put them in a saucepan with plenty of lightly salted water, the bay leaf, and the thyme. Bring to a boil, decrease the heat to a simmer, and cook for 15 minutes.

2. Add the finely diced vegetables and cook for another 5 to 10 minutes, until the lentils are tender; be careful not to overcook them. You'll know you overcooked them if you have dal instead of lentil salad.
3. While the lentils are cooking, make the dressing. Mix the vinegar, salt, mustard, oil, and shallot in a large bowl. You can use a tiny bowl, but you'll regret it.
4. Drain the lentils well and mix them into the dressing while still warm, stirring to coat the lentils. Remove the bay leaf and thyme and let cool to room temperature, stirring occasionally. When I stir things occasionally, I basically leave it there, forget about it, then remember a few hours later in a panic and think, "FUCK! I HAVEN'T OCCASIONALLY STIRRED ANYTHING!" Don't panic. The lentils will forgive you. Just stir the lentil salad.
5. Add some freshly ground pepper and mix in the parsley, nuts, and goat cheese. Taste, and add additional salt, if desired.
6. Eat it while warm or let it chill and eat it later. Maybe do both. It keeps for a couple of days in the refrigerator. Basically, it's good until it isn't. You'll know. Trust your gut.

Roasted Veggies

When You Want A Healthy Side Dish
Because Your Body Deserves Something Healthy

It may seem silly to add in Roasted Veggies as a recipe because they're so easy. But that's the point! THEY ARE SO EASY.

WHAT VEGGIES DO I USE?

What's sitting in your fridge that you thought you'd cook but never got around to?

I like baby carrots, parsnips, potatoes, beets, brussels sprouts. Fennel is great too.

Basically, heat your oven to 450°. Yes, 450°. Line a baking sheet with parchment. Or don't. You can live on the wild side and go without parchment. Toss your cut veggies with olive oil and liberally season with salt and pepper. Kick it up a notch and add some whole garlic cloves, or fresh rosemary or thyme.

The vegetables will cook and begin to caramelize. That's what you want to happen. You want to cook them until they're starting to get a deep golden brown. It can take 20 to 40 minutes depending on how big you cut your veggies.

I HAVE A BUTTLOAD OF ROASTED VEGGIES.

NOW WHAT?

The possibilities for these are endless. Serve them as a simple side dish. Bam. You're done.

Other options:

Add to your rice casserole.

Make an omelet and stuff with veggies and goat cheese.

Serve veggies over a scoop of couscous cooked in chicken stock. Add cashews and kalamata olives.

Make a burrito. Instead of stuffing it with meat, stuff it with these veggies, rice, and lots of cheese.

Serve over a bed of spinach and top with a vinaigrette, or a tahini dressing. Tahini dressing is really good.

Focaccia

When You Want Fancy Bread

FOCACCIA (FOH-KAHTCH-YAH) NO IT'S (FOH-KAH-CHA) OR MAYBE IT'S (FUHK IT IT'S BREAD)

I'm not going to lie to you. This recipe takes a shit ton of patience and commitment. But this recipe is worth it, because when you're done...oh, when you're done...you can sit and savor this bread, lick the salt and oil from your fingertips, take a taste of wine, and then put that fluffy bread against your lips and tongue...and...take a moment or two for yourself.

This is also great shared with someone else.

Stuff You Need

FOR THE BIGA: (Bee-gah. It's fun to say. Say it three times and twirl around. Nothing will happen, but maybe you'll laugh at being so ridiculous.) What is Biga? I think of it like an old witch that lives in the woods and stirs up trouble, but I tend to fantasize a lot. It's flour and water that you let ferment a bit for flavor. Not quite sourdough and not as fussy.
1-1/2 cups water, room temperature
1 packet instant dry yeast (2-1/4 tsp)
1 cup flour (or bread flour)

FOR THE DOUGH (Doh!)

Biga (see above)
2 cups flour (or bread flour)
2 tsps fine salt, or table salt (FLAVOR)
1/2 tsp sugar (to feed everything)

FOR THE TOP OF THE FOCACCIA

2 tablespoons fresh rosemary
4-5 tablespoons extra virgin olive oil
1/2 tsp coarse sea salt or kosher salt.

What You Do

1. Say a quick prayer to the universe that you have the patience to do this. Because you do have the patience! You've got this. Or you're getting it. In just four short hours.
2. Whisk the water and yeast together for the biga. Add the flour and whisk until smooth. Cover with plastic wrap and let it sit on your countertop for an hour to bubble. OR you can put it in the refrigerator and chill overnight while you sleep. If you do that, bring the biga to room temp for an hour or so before the next step.
3. Combine biga with 2 cups flour, 2 tsp fine salt and sugar in stand mixer with the dough hook. Mix on low until incorporated. Increase speed to medium-low and whisk for 5 minutes. For real! 5 minutes! You want the dough falling from the hook and not in a ball. Add a little

more water if you need to.

4. Put some olive oil in a bowl, pour the dough into the bowl and cover with plastic wrap. Let it rise for 1-1/2 to 2 hours, or until it doubles in size.

5. Grab a glass or metal 9x13 pan. Drizzle 3 tablespoons of olive into the pan and smear it around with your hands. You're playing! You're having fun! Life is good! Pour in the risen dough, pull gently so it fits the pan, and let it rise for another hour, until it's 1" thick. Cover with saran wrap. Be patient and let it rise that full inch. Because we all know that every inch counts, even when we pretend it doesn't!

6. Preheat oven to 400°.

7. Dip your fingertips into olive oil. Oh. Things are getting sexy in here. Now gently, GENTLY, press them into the dough to dimple it. You're making little divots in the dough that olive oil can soak into. Just do ten or fifteen or so, careful not to deflate the dough.

8. Drizzle dough with a shit ton of olive oil. Probably a few tablespoons. Sprinkle with kosher salt and rosemary.

9. Bake for 25 to 30 minutes, until the top is golden, it smells amazing, and the sides pull away from the pan.

10. Transfer the bread to a rack and cool 5 minutes before eating. I mean, slicing. Or, rip off a bit of the piping hot bread because you can't stop yourself and put it in your mouth where it will either burn you or just sizzle. You want care because the endorphins produced by eating fresh focaccia make everything nice.

11. Best eaten the same day UNLESS you're making Fancy Grilled Cheese Sandwiches with it.

12. Just eat the bread alone, or with Borsin cheese and a glass of wine, maybe some sundried tomatoes. Amazing served with homemade pasta.

Fancy Grilled Cheese Sandwiches

When You Want A Sandwich – Part Two

Sometimes, when I go grocery shopping, I like to imagine I'm on some cooking show and they say, "You have twenty minutes to gather your ingredients and then cook us something in five minutes that's so good we'll squeal."

This is that recipe. You can get everything at one of those giant warehouse stores, and then later when you're at home and want to squeal, you can either have an orgasm or make this sandwich.

Heck. Why not do both?

Just maybe not at the same time.

Stuff You Need

Sourdough bread, sliced
Mayonnaise
Boursin cheese
Artichoke hearts (marinated or not)
Kalamata olives, sliced and no pits
Sun Dried tomatoes, sliced
Pesto (Optional. This is Fancy Grilled Cheese Sandwich Level 11)

What You Do

1. Grab a cutting board and your bread. Lather bread with mayo. Yes. Mayo instead of butter. It's good. Trust me.
2. Flip bread over and now build your sandwich. Smooth on Boursin, then add artichokes, olives, and sun-dried tomatoes. You can even add pesto! Make sure the other side of the bread has Boursin too.
3. Heat your pan, tenderly and lovingly transfer your sandwich into the heated pan and cook until each side is golden. You may want to smoosh your sandwich with the spatula to make sure everything melts together.
4. Eat this sandwich with a side of root vegetable potato chips and a glass of wine. Because you're fancy.

White Bean Dip

When You're So Sick Of Hummus You Could Stab Yourself In The Eye With A Baby Carrot

When I lived in Traverse City, Michigan, until the age of ten or so, my mom had a house about two blocks from the bay. This was not a fancy house nor a prime location. We were poor and it showed in our house. My best friend lived one block over and next to a gas station and a mini mart.

The bay, though, was walking distance and I think living by the water seeped its way into my soul a little bit. Nothing calms me more than the sound of waves gently lapping the shore, the scent of rain rolling across the water, or the feel of cold sand between my toes.

Down the street from the bay was the Petoskey Shop and the Co-op. The Petoskey Shop was a dirty little store. Literally, dirt. It was just stones that this dude collected and polished. You can find Petoskey stones all over the beaches in Northern Michigan, and polished up they make great paper weights and jewelry. I'm still a little obsessed with them.

The Co-op was a unique store. Sometimes my friend and I would check it out. There was a bell that chimed when you walked in and a scent, that might have been carob chips or pot, slowly wrapped its arms around you.

The Co-op was run by a collection of hippies that still practiced free love and had all the hairstyles you can find in the original 1970s edition of The Joy Of Sex. Meaning, there was a lot of hair. And organic rock deodorant, maybe purchased from the Petoskey Shop.

There were grey garbage tubs filled with natural peanut butter, oats, or carob chips. There was a weird, dense bread; and things that smelled sort of bad and didn't taste much better. There were sometimes pot lucks with casseroles made with brown rice. Even the dessert casseroles were made of brown rice.

I hated this store. But I also loved it.

Maybe I'm telling this story because I ate a lot of this type of food at my Aunt Marilyn's when I'd babysit my cousin, Julia. It grew on me. Every now and then I crave a soy meatball on a bed of brown rice, sprinkled liberally with carob chips.

This next recipe hits the same I'm A Hippy spot in my heart. It's a spot that sometimes flares up, like a rash.

I made this for a Tanya Makes video and it was delightful. The dip was delightful; I'm not sure about the video. I thought the video was okay because I got to use my Ogre voices and that just doesn't happen every day.

This is super easy, quick, cheap, and it's good for you. Great with crudités but also with tortilla chips. And it's impressive because it's NOT hummus.

Stuff You Need

1 15 oz can cannellini beans, drained and rinsed
2 cloves garlic
2 tbsp fresh lemon juice
1/3 cup olive oil, plus 4 tablespoons
1/4 cup (loosely packed) fresh Italian parsley leaves
Salt
Freshly ground black pepper

What You Do

1. Pulse the garlic in a food processor. If you're angry, you can growl while doing this. It's fun!
2. Add the beans and the lemon juice into the food processor. Pulse until smooth, then add in your olive oil while running the processor until everything is nice and smooth. Add in your parsley and pulse again. There's a lot of pulsing with this recipe.
3. Add salt and pepper if you want and then eat the dip. Maybe you want to pour it into a platter and surround it with stuff so it's pretty. You can chill the dip or eat it warm. It's good both ways.

Morels: Two Ways

When You Want A Food Orgasm

If you have never had fresh morels picked from the woods, soaked in saltwater, and then fried in butter…you're missing out on one of the truly sublime food experiences. I see morels used in recipes all the time. In cream sauces. With beef. With chicken. And I always think WHAT THE FUCK ARE YOU THINKING? YOU'RE WASTING THOSE MORELS!

Don't eat them with something, eat them beautifully on their own. Make a recipe with something else. Like portabellas.

I was just going to post a recipe here, but I really have to talk about foraging for morels first, since it's sort of part of my favorite memories, my history, and has now worked its way into my DNA.

The woods of my youth were different than they are now. Can't you say that about a lot of things? Everything is different than it was in my youth. Or your youth. To THE youth.

Whatever.

I'm tired.

Anyway…

There was more open land, less trespassing signs, less gates and closed communities. The woods were denser and wilder, lusher, and more dangerous. In the spring in Northern Michigan, you could tell the health of a woods by walking into it. There were buds on the trees, a layer of brown dead leaves, a scent in the air of dirt; but a dirt that smelled like it was giving birth, because it was. Fiddlehead ferns poked out, ready to unfurl. And if you gathered them before it was too late, you could add them to your pasta for something that is like asparagus, but better.

Healthy woods felt alive, because it was. White trillium shivered in the wind close to the ground. Jack-in-the-pulpits poked out to you here and there. Beyond the scent of dirt and leaves and green things unfurling, you could taste fresh leeks on your tongue. This was the kind of woods we looked for around Mother's Day, when morels slowly erected themselves in the wood, their flesh earthy and musty and so phallic that I worried about falling on the ground and ending up pregnant.

We used to find morels in batches. We'd carry our paper lunch bags and our mesh bags through the woods. My aunts, uncles, and cousins. My mom and brother. And my grandparents—grandma lugging around her oxygen tank, grandpa with his jackknife and compass.

You had to get your Mushroom Eyes on before you could really hunt. Look at your feet as you walk, try to tell the difference between a folded leaf and a pointed mushroom cap. Usually, my uncle Dave would find one and then call all the kids over to re-find it. And once you'd found it, it was like your entire vision shifted and things previously invisible to you, shimmered their existence.

When you pick a morel, you pinch it off at the base, careful to leave its root. Morels are connected and a mystery. No one know quite how they grow, except you look for them where a fire has been, or on a mound of earth, in the valleys by a dead tree. You shouldn't find them in apple orchards or by pine trees, but we did, because everything was lush in the 80s.

There was a lot of darkness in my childhood, and a lot of Unknown. I never felt entirely safe or knew what the next day would bring. I was alone much of the time. But mushroom hunting with my family was the one thing I could count on. I knew we might not find any mushrooms at all, but I could always count on the searching.

It's that delight of searching that has stayed with me.

That, and the taste of a morel, hot from the pan, dripping with butter, nestled on my tongue and filling my mouth with a flavor that is hard to describe and harder to forget.

My grandma and mom taught me how to cook them, and I'll tell you how too. But don't pick mushrooms without a guide or someone to tell you that they're safe to eat. You could get the fake morels and those are poisonous. One way to tell is that if the mushroom looks like it's wearing a hat and is fibrous/cottony inside, that ain't a morel.

Morels: In Butter

What You Do

1. Cut morels in half so you can see the inside of them.
2. Place morels in a bowl of salted warm water. This will draw out any bugs or tiny worms. It's not usually an issue, but they are pulled from the earth, and the earth harbors a lot of creepy crawlies.
3. Dry morels gently with paper towel.
4. Heat a pan on the stove to medium high with a generous dollop of butter. Pour in half of your mushrooms.
5. Season with salt and cook until they just start to caramelize. They'll shrink, and that's okay.
6. Season with salt, and eat them right there, by the stove, as hot as you can bear it.

Morels: In Flour & Butter

What You Do

1. With the other half of mushrooms, put some flour in a plastic bag.
2. Add your slightly wet mushrooms and shake.
3. Cook in a medium high pan with plenty of melted butter. Cook until they're crisp and golden.

Hangover Hash Browns

When You Drank Too Many Martinis And Regret All Your Life Choices

I made a Tanya Makes video of this, and it's one of my favorites. Mostly because I really am hungover in it.

This recipe is sort of ridiculous and partly embarrassing. It's basically fried tator tots. IT'S ALSO REALLY GOOD! That may be the Midwesterner screaming in me, but sometimes Midwesterners are right.

Stuff You Need

Tater tots
Garlic Powder
Onion Powder
Lawry's Seasoning salt

What You Do

1. Pour those rock hard tater tots on a big plate and microwave them for about 90 seconds. You want them squishable. If you can't smash 'em, nuke them some more.
2. Heat a large pan and add in some olive oil or butter or olive oil AND butter. Once your tots are soft, mash them with a potato masher and pour them into the hot pan. The mashing is fun because it gives you something to focus on instead of how shitty you feel.
3. Once you have everything in an even layer, Sprinkle with garlic powder, onion powder and seasoning salt. It's okay to taste it to make sure you have the right blend of savory seasonings.
4. Now, just let those fuckers cook. Let them crisp and brown. It might take three or four minutes. Then you flip them and let the other side crisp and brown.

When you're ready to eat, just eat. Right from the pan.

Actually, don't eat from the pan. If you're hungover, your fine motor control probably isn't good and you could burn yourself.

Instead, put those crispy taters on a plate. Eat it like that or top with ketchup or sriracha, whatever you want to do that won't make you puke.

Drink some water. A LOT OF WATER.

Have a piece of toast.

Go back to bed.

Regret all your life choices and those terrible, terrible texts you sent last night.

But don't ever regret the hash browns.

Desserts

God, I love desserts. They're just…magical.

My friend Amy has a thing for desserts. Whenever I go out with her and share a meal, it's never "Are we going to have dessert?" it's "What are we going to have for dessert?"

At a restaurant where they had freshly baked chocolate chip cookies, that dessert became our appetizer. Then we ordered more dessert after our meal.

The perfect dessert reminds me of the perfect kiss: there's passion, it enflames you, it makes you moan, it steals your breath.

God, I love kisses like that.

I've had several of those kinds of kisses, and I'm going to tell you about one of them now because I am a fan of over-sharing.

THE MIAMI KISS THAT CHANGED MY LIFE

After I graduated college, my boyfriend and I moved to Miami. We were both in the Honors College at Grand Valley State University. Both of us had the same ACT scores. Both were strong writers, English majors, and same intelligence levels. He took all the courses you were supposed to take that studied the English canon. That is, lots of books by old dudes. Mostly books by old dudes. I took courses that focused in on women writers. I designed my own course with a professor so I could study Edith Wharton and Virginia Woolf. My boyfriend got a full ride to Miami, and I didn't get into any graduate schools. Seems the GRE really only tested your knowledge of those old dudes, and not women. My boyfriend got the full ride, and I worked at a café.

It was hard. He'd come home with his reading lists that I'd read after he was done with the books. He'd tell me about the parties he went to, and his class discussion, his papers. It was, literally, living with someone who was living your dream, and you weren't allowed to participate.

I worked at the café as a hostess and then a waitress. I was the only gringa there, and it was an experience that changed my life. There are so many stories I have about that experience, but I can't fit them all in here. I met people who were so different than the Midwesterners I knew. I was ice and they were fire.

After almost a year of living in Coral Gables while my boyfriend (who was by then my fiancé) went to school and I read Moby Dick on my lunch break at the café at the outdoor break table, I was depressed. Very depressed. My boyfriend had my life all mapped out for me. We would get married after he graduated. He'd become a professor and I could be a stay-at-home mom. We'd live in Detroit, close to his parents. The only thing was, I wanted to be a professor. I wanted to be a writer. I didn't want to be a stay-at-home wife in Detroit.

"But you didn't even get into grad school," he said kindly. It wasn't kind, but it was said in that way.

At the café, they'd have late night parties they'd invite me to. I couldn't go because my fiancé didn't like it. He didn't like me meeting people or doing things on my own. When he'd pick me up at work, he wouldn't come in. He'd just sit outside and wait.

"Why are you going to marry that guy? He's a controlling dick," said Christian. "You're what? 22 or something? You haven't even lived." Christian was working at the café while he got his real estate license. He was in his late thirties with silver hair, and he was fit, with bronze skin and bright blue eyes. He was beautiful. So was his brother Felipe. They had boundless energy and fought for every dime they made at that café so they could have a better life than they had in Cuba.

One night, in a fit of rebellion, I went to a party with all of the waitstaff. I told my boyfriend I was going, and there was so much anger pulsing through the payphone that I could feel it, even though he didn't say anything. "How are you going to get home?" he said. He owned the car and refused to pick me up. I told him I'd figure it out.

The party was okay. It was fun to get to know these people in a new way, but I still felt on the outside of everything. As it got later and later, I realized I needed to go home. I started to leave, planning on walking the mile or two home. Not a smart choice, but the only one I could make.

"Don't be ridiculous," Christian said. "I'll drive you."

He drove me back. It didn't take long. We had the windows down and I could smell the flowers that make the Miami air sweet. "Stop here," I said, about a block from my apartment. I didn't want to explain to my fiancé who was driving me home.

He pulled over and parked. The car ticked. "I just want to say one last thing about why you shouldn't marry this guy."

Before I could ask him what he meant, Christian leaned over and kissed me. It was a full- on kiss. One for the movies. I couldn't breathe, I didn't even know what to do at first. I had no doubt he'd stop if I wanted him to, but I didn't want him to stop. I just wanted to…I don't know…feel for a little bit.

He reached down and grabbed my hip and squeezed. It was the thickest part of my hip. The fat part. The part my fiancé was trying to get me to lose by running or working out more. Christian grabbed that part of my body and it was like he turned on all of me. I don't mean "I'm so turned on", I mean, I felt like I was without emotion or warmth, and he suddenly flipped the switch and I rushed into my body, this foreign vessel I'd been floating outside of.

I felt alive in a way I'd never experienced. It was such a weird thing, the feeling of an epiphany blossoming within me, triggered by his kiss.

The kiss didn't last long either. He pulled away and said, "And that's all I have to say on the matter."

I thanked him for the ride. I stumbled out of the car.

It wasn't necessarily the kiss that changed everything, but what the kiss symbolized: there was so much I was missing out on in my life.

The next day, I taped my engagement ring to my boyfriend's computer and I left for home…where I would one day become a professor. And a writer. And I would live my life with passion.

I never saw Christian again, but it was truly a kiss that changed my life.

A good dessert can be like that. It reminds you of how good it is to be in your body. How important it is to connect with loved ones. And maybe it inspires you a little bit to believe that there are sweet things in the world, just waiting for you to take a bite.

One Pot Brownies

When You Want Sexy Chocolate

Sarina Bowen and I wrote a book called MAN CUFFED. It's a standalone romcom, or you can read it as a part of the MAN HANDS series. Now, in Man Cuffed, there's a scene where they make brownies so good, they call them Moanies.

Because moaning after you eat good brownies is a real thing.

I made myself so hungry writing about Moanies, that I had to find an actual recipe that would do justice to it. Here is that recipe. After scouring the internet, I actually found this one on the inside of a bar of baking chocolate.

I made a video of me making these and then eating them. The music is so good. Moaning everywhere!

Stuff You Need

- 1 pkg. (4 oz.) BAKER'S Unsweetened Chocolate
- 3/4 cup butter or margarine
- 2 cups sugar
- 3 eggs
- 1 tsp. vanilla
- 1 cup flour
- 1 cup coarsely chopped pecans (or walnuts, or chocolate chips)

What You Do

1. Heat oven to 350°.
2. Line 13x9-inch pan with aluminum foil, with ends of foil extending over sides. Spray foil with cooking spray. (This is so when the brownies cool, you can easily lift them out and make a run for it so you don't have to share.)
3. Microwave chocolate and butter in large microwaveable bowl on HIGH 2 min. or until butter is melted. Stir until chocolate is completely melted. Stir in sugar. Blend in eggs and vanilla. Add flour and nuts; mix well. Pour into prepared pan.
4. Bake 30 to 35 min. or until toothpick inserted in center comes out with fudgy crumbs. (Do not overbake.) Cool completely. Use foil handles to remove brownies from pan before cutting to serve.

I actually cooked these for 30 minutes. They had a nice brownie 'skin' on them, but also a little wiggle. And then I spooned that piping hot brownie into a bowl and topped it with ice cream and it was like sex in a bowl. Like a volcano cake.

Then later, I tried the brownies cool when they had firmed up a little bit. And it was like sex in my hand. Or with my hand. It was dessert sex.

Then later, I used a two day old brownie, microwaved it until it was hot, put on more ice cream and IT WAS JUST AS GOOD AS THE FIRST TIME, BUT MAYBE BETTER BECAUSE I KNEW WHAT I'D BE GETTING THIS TIME.

Isn't that a lovely thing?

Alexander Cake

When You Want To Pretend You Have High Tea

It looks like a cake, but it tastes like a cookie and dissolves in your mouth. This is the prefect dessert for tea time.

Stuff You Need

- 1 lbs flour (3.5 to 4 cups)
- 1/2 tsp baking powder
- 1 lb butter, melted (1/2 salted, 1/2 unsalted)
- 1 cup sugar
- 1 cup seedless raspberry jam
- 1 cup powdered sugar
- 1-2 lemons

What You Do

1. In a small bowl, mix flour with baking powder well. Set aside.
2. In a larger bowl, melt butter and then mix in sugar.
3. Mix flour into butter a cup at a time til well blended.
4. Line a cookie sheet with parchment paper and spray. Spread dough to even thickness.
5. Bake 350° for about 30 minutes or until golden brown.
6. Cool completely.
7. Cut into two equal sections, so you have two squares.
8. When cool, spread jam on one layer and flip second layer on top. This requires some dexterity and a prayer.
9. Heat lemon juice with powdered sugar until melted. It'll be kinda thick. Add more sugar if it's too runny, or you don't like the tartness. (I happen to like the tart.)
10. Pour over cooled cake and smear it all over. It's probably best to do this with a spoon and not your hands, but who am I to judge?
11. Cut into squares and indulge.

This recipe was shared with me by Benita, and is a traditional Latvian recipe. Her dad made this, only he doubled the recipe.

Peanut Butter Cookies With Three Ingredients

When You Want Cookies NOW

This is the stupidest recipe out there because it's only three ingredients. By stupidest, I mean, the most brilliant. I've made this when I'm desperate for something sweet and also desperate to not leave my house and just use what I have on hand.

Stuff You Need

1 cup sugar
1 cup peanut butter
1 egg

What You Do

1. Preheat oven to 350°
2. Mix everything in a bowl. Scoop out a tablespoon of dough on ungreased cookie sheet.
3. Dip a fork in sugar and smoosh the dough til it's cookie-shaped. Smoosh it again crisscross way so you have a pattern on the cookie.
4. Bake for about 10 minutes.

Let them cool for a bit before you eat them. Or you can do what I do: try to eat the super hot cookie straight from the oven as it falls apart, but sigh with delight because once that steaming cookie hits your mouth…it's all pleasure. Also a little sizzle.

These Are Anne Of Green Gables Tarts, Motherfuckers

When You Want To Impress Your Literary Friends

I love *Anne Of Green Gables* so much. This series of books grounded me when I was a teenager. I felt a soul connection to the unwanted orphan who dreamed of being a writer, and I fell in love with the endearing and never scary Gilbert Blythe. I've always had a thing for smart guys and I think it started with Gilbert.

Some things you just never grow out of, I guess.

These tarts are cute and sweet and it's fun to tell people they're inspired from the *Anne Of Green Gables* books by Lucy Maud Montgomery. People will think you're smart if you cook something based on an actual book.

These little tarts, to me, taste like summer. Which is weird because they're made with frozen raspberries which you can get any time of the year.

Braid your hair, put on some puffy sleeves, sip some cordial and bake up these tarts.

Then Instagram the hell of it. People will give you all the likes, especially Canadians. There's nothing better than a like from a Canadian.

Stuff You Need

1 cup all-purpose flour	1 tbsp lemon juice
1 tbsp sugar	1 cup fresh raspberry
3/4 tsp salt	3 tbsp cornstarch
4 tbsp unsalted butter, chilled	1/4 cup cold water
1 egg yolk	1/2 cup sugar

What You Do

1. Preheat oven to 425°.
2. Combine flour, sugar, and salt in a large mixing bowl. Cut butter into flour mixture until it resembles tiny peas.
3. Combine egg yolk and lemon juice with a fork.
4. Sprinkle egg yolk mixture over flour mixture and stir together with a fork until it forms a ball. Refrigerate until ready to use.
5. Combine cornstarch and cold water in a small saucepan until smooth. Stir in sugar and raspberries. Cook and stir over medium-low heat until thickened, about 10-15 minutes. Allow mixture to cool. You'll probably have extra jam left over. Use it for something else, like

toast.

6. Remove dough from refrigerator and roll 1/8" thick. Cut tart shapes with biscuit cutter or top of cup. Place tart shells in prepared muffin tin.
7. Spoon filling evenly into tart shells, filling each no more than 2/3 full.
8. Bake at 425° for 10 minutes. Reduce heat to 350° F and bake for an additional 10 minutes or until pastry is golden brown.
9. Remove from oven and cool, in pans, for 15 minutes.
10. Remove from pans to cooling racks and cool completely.

Reddi-Wip From The Can

WHEN YOU'RE SO HAPPY YOU JUST CAN'T CONTAIN IT

Sometimes, you just need a dessert and STAT! Because you're happy. And you want instant gratification.

That's when I reach for the old Reddi-Wip!

What You Do

Shake the can up and press that Reddi-Wip valve straight into your mouth until your cheeks inflate with whipped cream.

Really inflate those cheeks.

That's what makes this fun.

1. Inflate.
2. Swallow.
3. Repeat.

Every Day Is Sundae

When You Want An Ice Cream Sundae But You're Too Embarrassed To Order One In Public

People who find solace in comedy usually do so to soothe some sore spots. I could tell you about the whole growing-up thing, and I've already told you much of it. Here is the condensed version:

I had a marimba playing father who chose the love of his 2nd wife over the safety of his kids. She had multiple personality disorder in the 80s and 90s, but that may have been because it was popular on Oprah at the time. She for sure had severe bipolar disorder and was mentally and physically abusive. I split time between their house and my mom's house, until my mom just couldn't parent me and then I went to my dad's house full time from 13 until 18. My stepsister and I were on suicide watch for my stepmom and there was all sorts of drama with that. Life was constantly scary and I never felt safe or loved or seen. At 18, my dad decided he'd had enough of parenting. He'd done his job. They kicked me out of the house. I managed to put myself through college; but there was no backup plan, no safety net for me. I'm still paying for both undergrad and graduate school. Out of five kids, I'm the only one to make it through college.

In 2001, I moved to NYC, got a job at Carnegie Hall and was there for 9/11. I had no friends or family there and no money at the time, and it truly shifted something inside me.

And there's all sorts of other sadness and messed up relationship stuff in my growing up, and the disappointments that happen and can make anyone bitter at some point.

But that story is not THIS story. THIS is a cookbook. Sort of.

Rest assured, I do have a number of really good memories from childhood.

Collecting pottery shards from the Bay in Traverse City. There were a lot of shipwrecks in that bay and shards would wash up on shore, smoothed by the sand. I loved imaging those last suppers aboard the ships (did they know it was a last supper), because in the tales I spun, the bay did not allow any survivors. (I've always been dramatic.)

I loved morel mushroom hunting with my family every spring and the random calls that would drift through the woods of "Ope!" or "Found One" and then we'd all run through budding woods to see if we could find more morels. They sometimes grow in patches.

I loved when my mom tucked me in with tuck tuck tuck tuck, all up and down my body. If I couldn't sleep, I'd curl under my Star Wars sheets with my flashlight and listen to the radio. I found a station that played BBC radio plays, and there was one about the end of the world that totally had me transfixed because there was a family together: A mom and a dad and a brother and a sister, and that was what I wanted more than anything, a family together, even at the end of the world.

And I also loved this sundae my mom would make for me sometimes. It's easy and so good, with a balance of flavors and textures I can now respect. Sweet and salty. Smooth and crunchy and creamy and gooey. Oh, the delight! The simple pleasure of being a kid and for a brief moment having all your wishes come true.

Stuff You Need

Hershey's Chocolate Syrup
(or hot fudge)
Vanilla Ice Cream
Banana
Spanish Peanuts (the kind
with the red skins)
Whipped Cream

What You Do

1. Load up a scoop or two of vanilla ice cream with sliced bananas.
2. Drizzle with Syrup.
3. Sprinkle with nuts.
4. Dollop with whipped cream.

Eat as is

…or you can make Ice Cream Soup by stirring and stirring and stirring until it becomes a lovely light chocolate color and is the consistency of soft-serve ice cream.

Eat. Breathe. Relax.

Life is good.

Volcano Sundae

When You Want To Level Up Your Ice Cream Sundae

Here's another ice cream dessert. This one I created while working at the Dairy Queen in Coopersville, Michigan. This was my second job. A step up from the Hardees across the street where I worked and would come home smelling like a giant ham.

At the DQ, I smelled like ice cream and hope, and that is a much better smell.

Anyway. I was hired by the manager who was a sophomore in high school, where I was a senior. He hired mostly girls that he liked, and that was okay with me. He was sweet. HE was also 300 pounds. This isn't a judgment. It's just he got a lot of crap for being a big guy and a manager at the DQ. He was super kind and also had a big heart. But yeah. He did hire girls he had a crush on, but he never took that too far. He just smiled. A lot. And there were a couple of guys he hired. We all became friends. We were an odd crew, sort of like the Breakfast Club of the DQ.

When I was hired, I had just graduated high school and it was the summer before I could escape Coopersville and Move On To Bigger Things. I was enrolled at the local college as part of their first Honors College, so I was pretty full of myself. I just wanted to make it through the summer and then get the hell out. Where better to do that than an ice cream shop?

The shift manager was in her thirties. A working mom. She wanted to become the manager but was pretty angry all the time and the higher up management thought she needed to work on her people skills. To do this, she posted signs everywhere telling us to wash our hands, clean the grille, make sure to cover the bananas.

I was fine with the signs. I just didn't like the misspellings or misplaced commas.

On slow days, I went around and corrected the misspellings on all the signs with a fat magic marker. Did I think I was helping? Nah. I didn't really think at all. The signs just bothered me. I remember one said: "It's you're mess. Clean it up." So I scribbled out the word YOU'RE, wrote YOUR and felt great satisfaction. Like I could breathe again.

I corrected all the signs without really thinking about it. All twenty-or-so of them.

Did the woman who wrote the signs think I was attacking her and putting her down? 100%.

When I came in for my next shift, she was just leaving, and she confronted me in the backroom by the punch clock and the bags of ice cream mix. "I'm going to kick your ass after work today. In the parking lot. High noon."

Maybe she didn't say high noon. Maybe I'm exaggerating. At any rate, she was serious. She had a tattoo and I'm pretty sure a switchblade.

On my shift, while singing along to Wham or Tears for Fears, I soothed my fear for the inevitable end of my life by creating this sundae.

She didn't kick my ass that day. She had to go pick up her kids and I snuck out the side door and ran to my car like a hunched-over coward. Who knew grammar could be so threatening?

Shortly thereafter, I quit and went to college.

I like to think that she got that managerial position. And I'm still sorry that I corrected her signs.

But at least I got this sundae out of the experience.

What You Do

1. Put a pool of hot fudge in your dish
2. Create a volcano on the pool of hot fudge with soft serve ice cream (or hard ice cream if you're at home)
3. Sprinkle with salted chopped pecans
4. Ladle over Chocolate Candy Coating until you've covered your ice cream and the shell hardens.
5. Eat it before someone kicks your ass.

Beaver Cake

When You Want To Make Something That Sounds Dirty But Isn't

I was on an episode of the Netflix competitive cooking series, *Nailed It!*. The holiday *Nailed It!*, Season 1, Episode 2: "Winter Blunderland". That whole experience…man. What a dream come true. And not just because I won $10,000. But also because I got to have fun while baking and practicing my improv skills. I also made terrific friends (I'm looking at you Brian and Lily and Laura), and to top it all off, I was awarded a 1980s Movie Moment with the classic slow clap. The pure slow-clap of the underdog winning, not the modern slow clap of disdain.

I came home overjoyed, smelling like cake, and hoping every day could be an episode on *Nailed It!*, or at least that they loved me so much, they'd invite me back to film…every new episode on *Nailed It!*

Alas, that did not happen.

So I decided to replicate the joy of Nailed It! by making a cake that I could tweet about. It would not be just any cake; it would be a cake with a double entendre. So I tweeted things like

"Hey guys! Come look at my beaver….

…Cake!"

And I laughed and laughed and laughed.

And then I filmed a video of me making the Beaver Cake and it's filled with stupid sex jokes…. but the thing is…no one seems to know that I KNOW those are stupid sex jokes. I got so many emails saying things like "Tanya, do you know that beaver is a term used for a woman's pubic hair?"

And then I laughed and laughed and laughed because, honey, I'm in my mid-forties. I know all about a woman's bush. Particularly mine.

This isn't a recipe really. You use cake mix and then you use frosting and decorate it.

Basically, make two layers of cake in small pans and then a third layer in a bowl. Frost the two regular cakes, and then invert the bowl cake on top of the two cakes, so you have what looks like a Minion. Then you decorate the whole thing with chocolate frosting, making sure to put some texture in your beaver hair. Fur. Beaver fur. Create eyes from marshmallows and chocolate. Cheeks from apricots. Then the fun part…create buck teeth from white chocolate, and a tail from a chocolate bar.

Then innocently ask everyone to come taste your beaver.

They'll love it.

Everyone should taste beaver at some point.

See?

The jokes are SO easy!!

Happy Endings

I don't really know how to end this cookbook, but I know I want it to have a happy ending. And, yes, I know that a happy ending has two meanings, one of which is culminating in an orgasm. And, yes, I want an orgasm. I've just reached the end of writing this weird little book, and I think I deserve one. I think YOU deserve one too!!

So after you finish this, please create a happy ending for yourself.

But allow me a few minutes first.

I just wanted to end with some thoughts on food and feelings. Yes, we shouldn't eat our feelings, but we should feel our feelings. And sometimes food can enhance those feelings, balance those feelings, or just intensify a moment. Sometimes food nourishes us, sometimes it helps celebrate us, and sometimes it connects us. Sometimes it can do all of those things at once.

I want to end with a final recipe that's for a cocktail. I love cocktails. Martinis especially. I love citrus and gin drinks and tiki drinks and bubbly champagne. I also love fruit cocktails without alcohol especially if there's a little fizz.

Here's a cocktail I tried when I was staying at a beautiful old rickety cottage on Lake Michigan. (I made a *Tanya Makes* video of it.) It was inspired by my friend Hillary, an awesome narrator and friend, who said this to me when I was obsessing about wanting to make a drink, but I wanted it to be good and festive and I didn't know if I could make something and on and on and on and she just said: "Just make the fucking drink. Pour in some juice. Pour in some vodka or tequila. Add some ice. It's a fucking drink."

I think this is a good philosophy for life. Don't overthink it. Just fucking make your life. It'll be festive because it's yours.

The Fucking Drink

Stuff You Need

Some grapefruit juice
Some vodka (I like
  grapefruit flavored
  vodka)
Some ice

What You Do

1. Shake together and pour into a martini glass, or serve over some rocks.

Then go find a sunset and send cheers to your loved ones, to yourself, and to new beginnings.

Much love,

Tanya

Acknowledgments

A huge thank you to David Kolenda for the countless hours he spent transforming Tanya's scrawls and random ideas into an actual book. The fonts and designs he came up with are just perfect. Thank you to Kim Hindman for her beautiful cover.

Tanya would also like to thank her friends for believing in her.

About The Author

Tanya Eby is the USA Today bestselling writer of the *Man Hands* series with Sarina Bowen. She is an award winning audiobook narrator and producer, and a former contestant on NAILED IT! HOLIDAY! on Netflix. Find her on various social media platforms or check out her occasional *Tanya Makes* videos on YouTube. She loves food, potlucks, classic movies, horror stories, and lives in Michigan with her kids.

You can also find Tanya on all the social media outlets including:

@Blunder_Woman

www.facebook.com/TanyaEbyNarrator

https://bit.ly/TanyaMakes

Blunder Woman Productions produces a wide array of books and audiobooks in nearly every genre including multiple award-winning narrations.

Visit www.blunderwomanproductions.com today to find your next favorite book!

BLUNDER
WOMAN
productions